I0438834

The State I'm In

The State I'm In

by

Andrew James

AuthorHouse™
1663 Liberty Drive
Bloomington, IN 47403
www.authorhouse.com
Phone: 1-800-839-8640

First published by AuthorHouse 4/7/2010

ISBN: 978-1-4184-9332-5 (e-book)
ISBN: 978-1-5872-1522-3 (Paperback)

Original Printing 7/6/01
1stBooks - rev. 04/01/10

Printed in the United States of America
Bloomington, Indiana

This book is printed on acid-free paper.

Prelude

There is no Federal agency more feared by the majority of American people than the Internal Revenue Service (IRS) and with good reason. This agency has the power to intrude, persecute, and ruin the lives of ordinary citizens. They possess the supremacy to tax, penalize, incarcerate, and destroy their adversaries. More than any other administration in history, the Clinton regime has harnessed all the terror of that agency and directed it against its political enemies (I.e. Lewinsky, Tripp, Jones, Me, & others). In a very real way, the IRS has been the Clinton's secret police agency. They are the strong-arm guys utilized when no other punishment or coercive measure is possible. As the author of this mini-novel, I too have fallen prey to this Clinton and United States Government method of attack.

On December 8, 2002, I mailed a copy of this book (1st edition) to New York State Senator Hillary Clinton, Washington, D.C. In my cover letter, I requested that she do all in her power to help minimize government intrusion and taxes in the lives of those New York State citizens and businesses she represents as State Senator. On January 14, 2003, I received a pleasant letter from Hillary Rodham Clinton on United States Senate, Washington, D.C. letterhead thanking me for including her in the distribution of my work. Only eight business days prior, I received an IRS audit letter demanding an audit review of the past years' tax records. – I guess she didn't like my ideas of smaller government and fewer taxes. It was the first time I've been audited in fifty-years of life. Only an idiot would attribute this to coincidence. Especially when it turns out that her upstate New York office is only one door down from the IRS office in the Syracuse, New York Federal Building.

Because many of the scenes in the book were located in the State of Ohio, I also sent a copy to Ohio Governor Bob Taft. But, since my book complains about large government and excessive taxes, his office also answered me with a tax audit notice, even though I've never been a resident of the State of Ohio. These State and Federal audits were drawn out to a point where I eventually lost my job, was financially ruined, and have still not recovered. I have copies of letters, IRS and State audit correspondence, post-marked envelopes, eviction, and bankruptcy notices to substantiate my claims. In the end, I won my battles and was vindicated as a prudent and accurate filer, but my family lost the war against an abusive U.S. Government. I now agree with author Barbara Ehrenreich who so deftly states that the American dream is truly one of 'bait and switch' in her book of the same title. We are brainwashed in our schools that Americans are free to express themselves, free to challenge governmental leaders without persecution, and free to better our lives via strong work ethic and college education, but this is a mirage for most. Despite the U.S. Tax Reform Act of 1976, and the U.S. Congress amendments to Section 6103 of the Internal Revenue Code which forbids the use of tax agencies as coercion and retribution arms of government, I have evidence that they still are. United States tax authorities continue being manipulated by politicians for use as investigatory and prosecutorial arms of government though these abuses of power have been against the law since 1976. As seen during 1994 Senate hearings regarding ongoing political IRS abuse, there are millions of other hard-working U.S. citizens who have also felt the sharp sword of censorship swung by the strong arm of the IRS since the 1976 laws and regulations were implemented. Sorrowfully, I argue that our country is not the free democracy we are brainwashed to believe in. The lesson I should learn from my life story and my research for this work is that Americans must, 'put up and shut up.' But at the risk of further persecution, I forge ahead with the distribution of this book because I feel it's a story that must be communicated in hopes that it will help enact significant corrective change from our current exponentially accelerated government growth tact. I feel compelled to add my story to others, in hopes of enacting that change. Change toward increased individual and corporate freedom. Change toward fewer taxes and less government intrusion in the lives of American citizens. Change in direction from adversarial political attitudes towards business owners. And change from our Country's current course toward socialism and communism to one that again favors capitalism and individual freedom. America is, after all, supposed to be a capitalistic democracy not a socialistic or communistic state. –At least that's what our children are programmed to believe in our State run schools.

Andrew James
PO Box 884
Cortland, NY 13045

December 8, 2002

Senator Hillary Clinton
476 Russell Senate Office Bld.
Washington, DC 20510

Dear Senator Clinton:

While you were running for the New York State Senate Seat, you had conducted a "listening tour" in upstate New York. I never received word (via the media) of what you heard, but the enclosed book is what people in **upstate** New York are talking about and I thought you might like a copy.

This book gives an insight into the minds of rural upstate New Yorkers', like me. I hope this book will give you an idea of why hard-working upstate New York citizens feel so strongly against government intrusion and high collective tax rates. --Thank you for your help in these areas.

Yours truly,

Andrew James
Author

www.AndrewJamesNPM.com

Internal Revenue Service

Department of the Treasury

Date: January 2, 2003

PO Box 884
Cortland, New York 13045-0884

Taxpayer Name:

Taxpayer Identification Number:

Tax Form:
1040

Tax Period(s):
2001

Person to Contact:
(Appointment Secretary)

Employee Identification Number:
16-

Telephone Number:

FAX Number:

Dear Taxpayer:

The purpose of this letter is to let you know that I have scheduled the following appointment to meet with you and examine the above referenced tax return:

Place: PO Box 884
Cortland, NY 13045-0884

Date: Please Call Back Within

Time: 10 Days for Appointment

Should you need to change this date, please contact me to arrange a more convenient meeting. I will consider the above appointment confirmed if I don't hear from you by January 13, 2003

In order to minimize the time we need to complete the examination, please have available the items listed on the attached Form 4564, *Information Document Request*, at our first appointment.

You may have someone represent you during any part of this examination. Should you want someone to represent you, please give us a completed Form 2848, *Power of Attorney and Declaration of Representative*, at our first meeting. We will delay examination activity to allow you time later to secure a representative if you choose.

We encourage you to read the enclosed Publication 1, *Your Rights as a Taxpayer*, and Notice 609, *Privacy Act and Paperwork Reduction Act*. Thank you for your cooperation.

Sincerely yours,

Internal Revenue Agent

Enclosures:
Publication 1
Notice 609
Form 4564

Letter 2205 (D 10-1999)
Catalog Number 63

HILLARY RODHAM CLINTON
NEW YORK
SENATOR

RUSSELL SENATE OFFICE BUILDING
SUITE 476
WASHINGTON, DC 20510-3204
202-224-4451

United States Senate

WASHINGTON, DC 20510-3204

January 14, 2003

(3)

Mr. Andrew James
Post Office Box 884
Cortland, New York 13045

Dear Mr. James:

Thank you for sending me a copy of your book, *The State I'm In*. You were very thoughtful to include me in the distribution of this werk.

With appreciation, I am

Sincerely yours,

Hillary Rodham Clinton

Hillary Rodham Clinton

(Andrew James, Pseudonym)
Park Ave West
Mansfield, OH 44902

March 23, 2002

Governor Bob Taft
30th Floor
77 South High Street
Columbus, OH 43215-6177

Dear Governor Taft:

Ohio taxes are incessantly escalating as illustrated in many issues of this year's Mansfield, Ohio and Columbus, Ohio newspapers. It would be helpful if your office could determine ways to cut unnecessary spending, thereby saving money for Ohio's over-taxed citizenry

Please accept the enclosed copy of my latest novel entitled, "The State I'm In" which is a fictional story based on actual events. Many of the issues, in this novel, are based upon my experiences in Ohio. In the story, I explain that the collective tax rate (for Ohio) has risen to consume 59.1 percent of the income of Ohio taxpayers. While your office continues to pitch the media and citizenry for increases in their collective tax rate, I would argue that that rate is already abusive, excessive, and counterproductive

Any thing that you could do to decrease the collective tax rate would be appreciated. –I hope you enjoy the complementary issue of my book that will explain, in detail, why I argue that the collective Ohio tax rate is too high. Please help cut taxes and wasteful government spending in Ohio.

Sincerely Yours,

(Andrew James, Pseudonym)
Author

Enc.

NPM II COMPANY

New York Office
PO Box 884
Cortland, NY 13045
Ph: 607
Fax: 607

Ohio Office
Park Avenue West
Suite 208
Mansfield, OH 44902
Ph: 419 525-
Fax: 419 52 7

Author/Composer
(Andrew James, Pseudonym) www.AndrewJamesNPM.com

Income Tax Audit Division
P.O. Box 182847
Columbus, Ohio 43218-2847
www.state.oh.us/tax/

April 11, 2002

(5)

P.O. Box 884
Cortland, New York 13045

Dear Taxpayer:

We are currently reviewing your 2001 Ohio income tax return which reflected an overpayment of $2,153.00. Your refund will be delayed until we have completed this review.

To "speed up" this process, would you please provide us with a photocopy of your 2001 New York state tax return(s). After our review of this information, we will advise you of our findings in writing.

The above information should be forwarded in the enclosed envelope within 30 days of this letter's date. No consideration can be given to your refund/credit without providing this information.

Income Tax Audit Support Unit
FAX (614) 433-7844

Enclosure
KET/kjg

PA/[illegible]-16
6,9[illegible]7,044

STATUTORY EMPLOYEE
WORKING OUT OF STATE.

About The Book

Andrew James writes about the wretched life of an individual taxed too heavily by an abusive and excessive U.S. government. The main character of the story, Andrew Henry, resides in rural upstate New York and in his diary he writes: "In a capitalistic society, the government should create and enforce laws, not redistribute the wealth. To give to one person, it must take from another, and for average income earners and the working poor, this burden is too great. The U.S. government has become a socialist regime, as opposed to a capitalistic state, and its quest for control of America's money has elevated its involvement in the economy to a level that borders on communism. Not only is the government's extreme redistribution of wealth unfair, it should be illegal since the current collective tax rate of 59.1 percent infringes on the dreams, ambitions, and desires of working families and individuals (see pp. 14 & 15). Also, the designed inequities of the American tax system discriminate against, and persecute, certain citizenry. In the United States of America, discrimination in any form should be illegal."

Later in the story, America is attacked by a substantial multinational invasion force. Henry finds shelter in an Ohio fallout shelter while his wife and daughter find shelter in an upstate New York fallout shelter. The many countries harboring past grievances with the United States strike with surprising strategic planning and accuracy. While in the shelter, Henry is protected from the fallout generated from this limited nuclear attack. Henry describes the shelter construction and protective qualities.

This book offers a scholarly insight to the culture of rural upstate New York and other American communities that feel overwhelmed by our current tax system. It also lends insight to where we may be heading, as a peace-loving nation, in a militarily volatile world.

IT IS A "MUST READ" FOR:

Politicians
Military Personnel
Scholars
Every U.S. Citizen.

THE STATE I'M IN

Introduction

"The state I'm in is the state of poverty. The state the patrons at the corner gas station are in is a state of disgust over an abusive government. And the state the government is in is New York. Sure, I have acquired a lot of 'things' in my life, but I still consider myself poor. You see, when you don't have a family able to support you financially after high school, every expense puts you into debt. And my mountain of debt has grown to an intolerable level over a lifetime of needs." --Andrew Henry Diary, October 19, 2003.

So begins the physical and intellectual journey of the main character in Andrew James's novel, The State I'm In. This story places an American citizen named Andrew Henry into shoes similar to those worn by the downtrodden characters of an old-English Charles Dickens novel, such as Hard Times, A Tale of Two Cities, and David Copperfield. It also possesses many of the same criticisms referenced in past political exposé novels like 1984 and Animal Farm by George Orwell.

In his quest to earn enough income to pay his numerous New York State taxes, Henry must leave his family and find work in Canada, Vermont, Pennsylvania, and Ohio, to keep the New York State government from repossessing his home. During his travels, Henry finds cities enjoying racial harmony, cities doing away with the industrial revolution giants of the past, and he finds himself. He discovers the world has changed from the picture painted for him in his youth, and he finds a place where honest men, such as he, can find peace. That place is known to us all, and it is exposed within the many thought-provoking pages of this novel.

If you are interested in understanding the burdens of average Americans, if you want to better understand the perspective of an enraged taxpayer, and if you can tolerate frankness in the pursuit of truth, then read on and be enlightened to the plight of the working poor on American soil.

"Heart wrenching, political, and educational."
NPM II Publishing Company

"The story reads like a modern-day version of Death of a Salesman, Great Expectations, and Animal Farm combined into one."
NPM II Publishing Company

"An interesting socio/political commentary."
NPM II Publishing Company

Dedication

This novel is dedicated to the liberals who dare to read on, at the risk of becoming enlightened.

From their understanding, the specters of hope and liberty shall arise.

Andrew James

THANK YOU

Thank you to my friends in New York City, Syracuse, Truxton, Otisco Lake, and Weedsport, New York for their inspiration. Thanks are also extended to my graphics friend in Mansfield, Ohio.

List of Characters

Andrew Henry	The Main Character
Laurence O'Loughlin	Service Station Owner
John Martin	Logging Company Owner
Judith Bucci	Physical Education Teacher
Kelly Henry	Daughter of Andrew Henry
Carol Henry	Andrew's Wife
Chad Garchow	Andrew's Brother-in-Law
Grandma	Carol Henry's Mother
Grandpa Ed	Carol Henry's Step-Father
Joyce Albright	Carol Henry's Cousin/ Teacher
James Dee	Retired College Professor
Marsha Whitten	Guidance Counselor
Richard (Dick) Whitney	Retired Air Force Colonel
Alan Whitten	Retired Postal Employee
Jacob Whitten	Public Television Station Pres.
Mr. Finestine	The Boss at NPM Paper
Kurt Henderson	V.P. of Trade Relations at NPM
Chas Gallo.	Colleague at NPM Paper
Paul Commings.	Colleague at NPM Paper
John Cindrich	Owner of Cindrich Paper and a Retired Military Col.
Sharon Cindrich	John's Wife
Debbie Cindrich	John's 6 Year-Old Daughter
Michael Cindrich	John's 3 Year-Old Son
Jim Fletcher	Warehouse Foreman
Dan Cindrich	John's Brother
Susan Cindrich	Dan's Wife
Mrs. Cindrich	John's 85 Year-Old Mother
Mrs. Long	Mrs. Cindrich's Caretaker
Sam Thompson Radio Operator	Rochester, N.Y.Short-wave
Lieutenant White	Militia Cell Commander, Clawson, N.Y.
Dick Cunningham	Stonewall, N.Y. Friend

Geographic Areas

Durham County	The County of Andrew Henry's Upstate N.Y. Residence
Decorah, OH	The Town of Andrew Henry's Ohio Residence/Office
Ashwood County	The County Location of Andrew's Ohio Residence/Office
Wellsville, OH	The Town the Cindrich's Family Farm is in.
Patton, OH	The Town the Cindrich's Paper Company is Located In.
Clawson, NY	The Site of the Upstate N.Y.Militia Fallout Shelter

Contents

"At what point does capitalism become socialism, and democracy a dictatorship?"

Andrew Henry's diary dated October 19, 1998
written at 43 and 1/2 years of age.

Chapter One: The Condition

Located within the still and obscure southern foothills of the vast Adirondack Mountain Range lies a small valley speckled with pristine pastures, immense wood lots, and the homes of 236 hard-working inhabitants. Although the view from the eyes of the crows now flying high overhead with the rising sun would be peaceful and breathtaking to any human observer, the true essence of this valley is dramatically different from the seemingly peaceful presence exhibited now. I know this town of my birth and my great-great-grandfather's birth intimately, and I sense an uneasiness rising within its borders, and within my soul, at this fog-laden early morning hour of 5:00 A.M.

At the heart of town, and an easy walk from my residence, lies a service station that is already characteristically bustling with the 'news of the day'. As I enter, the proprietor, Laurence O'Loughlin, is seen sitting hunched over his desk located behind the service counter. As usual, for this time of the morning, he is diligently scribbling out bank drafts in an attempt, I presume, to keep one step ahead of his many creditors. As I pass, his head pops up from his work and with a hurried, yet cordial, "mornin' Andrew," his eyes and concentration simultaneously return to his pile of payables as I emit a corresponding greeting launched to the echo of the door slamming shut with its bells ringing behind me.

Enroute to the coffee counter I pass three patrons dressed in dirty, work-stained clothes and offer a quick and unimposing; "good mornin'," while they continue their discussion of a; '*Miss. Judith Bucci*'. I am familiar with the topic to which they speak. It is one that has already addressed itself to me, in a painful way, in last evening's news print. This '*Miss. Judith Bucci*' is the Grifton Junior High School girls' physical education teacher. She is gay, she has purple hair, and she is as outspoken and opinionated as any in our county. These, though, are not the traits that inspire the wrath against her that is emanating from this early morning group of three. It was her recommendation in yesterday's Post-Gazette News that voters in the county approve the upcoming school tax increase of 38 million dollars that has brought her their attention in conversation, ...their disdain, ...and their wrath!

"Where in tar-nation does she think we're gonna' come up with that kind of money," states John Martin, a hard-working owner of a local logging company. From the window, John's rig can be seen idling outside at the diesel pump as he talks. The rig is ready for another twelve-hour day of work. --Just one more twelve-hour day, in a lifetime of twelve-hour days, for John. The other two persons, one an owner of an underground power line installation company and the other an owner of a utility pipeline installation company, laugh in agreement with John and quickly chime in. Laurence stands up from his paper work and joins in the conversation.

"Businesses are moving out at a record rate in this God forsaken state and the gosh-darn government officials still keep increasing our taxes," he says. "When are they gonna' dog-gonnit' realize they're ruining this state by taxing us too much?"

As the murmur of the room fades into nothingness in my mind, I walk to the cash register reflecting on my plight. One cup of coffee, --fifty cents. I'll have enough until Thursday's paycheck to buy one cup of coffee, plus a breakfast treat each day, and that will give me the energy to phone my many customers for orders and aggressively plow through a mountain of paper work. Without this breakfast diversion from my work-related anxieties, and without the energy this nourishment will bring, I could not 'buck up' and conquer the aggravating day's work at hand.

"One dollar and twelve cents!" O'Loughlin's voice jolts me back to reality.

"Oh, thanks," I respond. In my day-dreaming I hadn't realized that I had mechanically picked up a cheese-filled danish on the way to the register.

"Yep," O'Loughlin retorts," fifty cents for the coffee, fifty cents for the danish, and another eight cents for our beloved government!"

The state I'm in, is the state of poverty. The state the patrons at the corner gas station are in, is a state of disgust over an abusive government. And the state the government is in, is New York. Sure, I have acquired a lot of *'things'* in my life, but I still consider myself poor. You see, when you don't have a family able to financially support you after high school, every expense puts you into debt. And my mountain of debt has grown to an intolerable level over a lifetime of needs.

As the dawn fog lifts, and the beams of the sun to the east find crevices around my window from which to penetrate into my upstairs office, I rise from my desk to open the curtains. Two stories beneath me, I can see our two dogs frolicking in the back yard. Beyond them and towards the rising early morning sun, lies a meadow with two deer bounding away. Their white tails can be seen dancing to and fro as they pop up, and over, each obstacle in their random path. Then, with a seemingly effortless bound, they simultaneously leap over a barbed wire fence and are gone. My youngest dog barks to get my attention and as my eyes return to the scene directly below, I yell through the window pane, "get going," with a gentle chuckle. She looks at me with a nod of understanding, then turns and darts away to catch her mate now in the meadow barking at the disappearing deer.

Like O'Loughlin at the corner store, I too am plagued with a desktop of paper work, though mine will not be one of debt reduction today, since the funds needed for that task will be unavailable until my next payday. Rather, my pile consists of general business paper work. I have accounting ledgers to complete, bid rebates to report, survey results to tabulate, and orders to process and fax to my company by 7:30 A.M. As I glance at my office clock I can see that the hour of 7:00 A.M. has already passed so I hurriedly return to my chair and begin faxing completed orders to my company headquarters before the 7:30 A.M. deadline for 'next-day business' arrives. With the arrival of 7:30 A.M. I have entered all my orders and, after 2 1/4 hours of intense paper work, am ready for a short break. As I lean back into my office chair, I take an unintentional sip of my now cold coffee and begin to reflect on my life as I regretfully swallow. Cold, I think. --Just like my coffee, my life has turned out to be cold and difficult to swallow. This house, located only a block down from the service station I left almost two hours ago, has turned from shangri-la to nemesis as it continues to erode faster than I can find the funds to repair it. My wife and daughter are pleasantly pleased with the premises, while I have endured a decade of *embittering* renovations all completed through the hard work of my own carpentry prowess and accompanied with my overwhelming drive not to be defeated by this old, 1935 era, decrepit, yet still regal, house. I say *'embittering'* because in addition to the obvious pains and wear inflicted on my physical bearing over many years of harsh nocturnal and weekend labor, an unwelcomed and unaffordable increase in property taxes was the unfortunate *real* result of my struggles.

"Darn you!" was my reaction to the tax appraisers when they had arrived, two years ago, requiring that I let them into my home to evaluate my renovations. Renovations completed solely by me, my wife, and my daughter after five long years of hard work.

"We are with the County Tax Office," they had said, "and we've been sent over to re-assess your property tax value". I remember their words well, and as the two government intruders had entered my home, they immediately bore my wrath.

"What have either of you two done to come in my home and require me to pay you more in taxes? Neither of you have invested money into materials, so you have no vested interest. Neither of you have lived in squalor like my wife and daughter have while we worked on this decrepit house, one room at a time, over a five year-period. Nor has either of you invested time into this property. What right, therefore, do you two have swooping in here like vultures on a kill attempting to snatch extra money from my already depleted purse? Extra money you have done ABSOLUTELY nothing to earn! You have invested nothing over the past five years and now you demand money. FOR WHAT!" I had exclaimed with my voice rising with each word uttered.

"Just doing our job, calm down. Re-assessment of property values is always required after renovations are completed."

"Who told you about my renovations!" I had exclaimed with passion as one of the investigators walked room to room taking measurements and writing notes. "What were you two doing over the last five years, driving through town and looking for building materials in my driveway or something? Or was it one of your fellow bureaucrats in town, perhaps the dog catcher, or the town clerk that turned you onto me?"

"Look Sir, we are only doing our jobs," the one I'll now call '*bureaucrat inspector #1*' had replied. "If you have an objection, you may call the number on this card." As he handed me his card I remember him stepping back a step while I read it. It simply had the County Tax Commissioners mailing address and phone number. A well-prepared card it was although the edges were a bit bent and worn due, I'm sure, to its frequent use with other disgruntled and abused taxpayers over a duration of many years.

"You two and your 'commissioner' should be disgusted with yourselves," I responded after reading their card. "You swoop down on my private property in the guise of American Eagles but you are nothing but loathsome vultures! Despicable, disgusting, VULTURES!" At that moment I had to excuse myself from their presence, in disgust, and exit my home for I had become too enraged to further tolerate their presence. Leaving them alone to compute their increased tax assessment of my premises, I stormed out of the room without a further word. I knew that any further attempt to influence their resolve in increasing my property taxes, would be in vain. The tax increases they have planned for me will take additional and unavailable money out of my family's pocket for the remainder of our stay in this dwelling, I remember thinking. As I sat on the front steps of my home, I also mentally reflected on how unfair it seemed to me that they were inflicting even more pain and burden on my already overtaxed personage. While my wife, daughter, and I had done all the work and spent our own money to do <u>necessary</u> renovations to this old house, the two inside and their 'commissioner' had done nothing to help. Oh yes, they hindered with building permit fees and costly zoning regulation requirements. They had required certified waste haulers to haul our demolition scraps to certified landfills where they could charge us their extra *'dumping fee tax'*. BUT THEY DID NOTHING TO HELP AND THEY WERE SNOOPING AROUND LIKE JACKALS LOOKING FOR AN EXCUSE TO EXTRACT MORE MONEY FROM MY FAMILY'S ALREADY MEAGER PURSE. The fees and regulations they had imposed during our renovation process were simply their way to "red flag" my house for a future re-assessment and property tax increase after my renovations had been completed. They are like the *'thought police'* in George Orwell's book 1984, I remember thinking at the time.

The result of their assault on my personage was an increase in my property taxes of $1,500 per year. Now $1,500 per year doesn't sound too overwhelming until you consider that is based on my *net* earnings as opposed to my *gross* earnings. Given that 43.3% of my gross paycheck goes to payroll taxes *(refer to page 14)*, that means that I will have to earn an extra $2,645.50 each year to pay for the extra $1,500 levied against me for my home improvement. *(I.e. $2,645.50 gross pay less 43.3% deducted for my combined payroll taxes = $1,500.00 net earnings available for spending).* If I was not able to pay this additional 'extortion fee' my home would be in default and auctioned at a government auction sale. If the auction price did not match the outstanding mortgage due and back taxes owed, I would be responsible for the difference. This sum could be attached as a lien against future earnings from both my wife's job and mine. In this government dictatorship of America, we had no resolve but to pay this extra extortion fee. To pay this fee I would simply have to work longer and harder hours. The property tax arm of our taxing services is an agency accountable only to itself. It is an agency that is completely out of control, since many of the votes to increase property tax rates come from those in our community who rent as opposed to those who own property. Through their abusive tax policies, their structure unavoidably ensures that only people of wealth or high-paying jobs obtain the decent homes in America. Struggling people like myself could afford a nice home if it weren't for the unfair and heavy tax burdens levied against us. Home ownership and maintenance could be affordable if it were not for abusive property taxation. Since that meeting with those two bureaucrats from the *'dictators office'*, two years ago, the government has been my arch rival and nemesis. But in order for me to pay them this year's increased extortion fee, I must return my thoughts to the more immediate adversary still lying on my desk before me, which is a mountain of paperwork awaiting my attentive return.

This adversary of time-consuming office paper work must be conquered by 9:00 A.M. You see, it is by the hour of 9:00 A.M. that most of the buyers at the fifty-three companies I sell my coarse paper products to will have already organized their work load. They will have already obtained their second cup of coffee for the day. And they will now be ready for an onslaught of phone calls, including those from salesmen like me peddling new products, offering product 'deals' and 'promotions', and/or returning their prior phone calls regarding a vast array of common customer inquiries. All of this communiqué to be accomplished by fax, by computer, and by phone.

"Dad, gotta' go to school. Bye, love ya', have a good day."

My fourteen-year-old daughter Kelly storms into my office with her usual exuberance, hugs me around the neck and kisses me on the cheek. Next, with the same exuberance as her energetic entry, she begins her departure. Upon reaching the door and flinging it open, she turns. "How do I look?" she asks.

"Magnificent!" I respond. "You look great! You always look great!"

She whirls, --and is off.

It is now 9:00 A.M.; and with the day's paper work conquered, or at least diminished to a tolerable level, I begin my rampage of phone calls. Using two phones, I can begin dialing a second customer while concluding the conversation with the customer on the first telephone line. While this process continues through mid morning, I begin to reflect how I would rather be out calling on these accounts in person. But, since I have already spent this month's budget for travel expenses, I am now relegated to only conducting business by phone until my next paycheck arrives on Thursday. Thank God for the third Thursday of every month. It is this third 'Thursday' that I finally receive my straight-commission paycheck for the month, a check that has paid my expenses every month for twenty years. Unfortunately that check never provides a savable surplus against the un-daunting onslaught of expenses, bills, and taxes that keep me in debt; keep me working; and has given recent rise to the concept of giving up completely. Oh, I never thought this way before. No, I was raised with the notion that if you worked hard and managed your debts well, anyone could be successful.

Now at forty-three and a half years of age, I am forty years wiser, three years over my head in debt, and half in the grave. As my health continues to erode, so do my dreams of conquering my mountain of debt. And with the constantly increasing number of government employees like *Judith Bucci* all relentlessly asking for, and receiving, more and more funds through increased taxes, so go my ideals and hopes. But, enough of this digression, it is time to re-address my workload.

"Sanity and insanity are defined by the eyes of the beholder,and those eyes become less judgmental with age and experience."

Andrew Henry's diary dated November 26, 1998.
Thanksgiving.

Chapter Two: Thanksgiving

It is now November, and God has provided us with a wonderfully classic Thanksgiving day. The weather is cold, overcast, and tranquil outside my mother-in-law's quaint home located on the east shore of Peck Lake, New York, while the atmosphere remains warm, cozy, and bustling with activity on the inside. This annual Thanksgiving pilgrimage to 'Grandma's' house is a special event for my wife and daughter. They've come dressed for the occasion in the latest fall-fashions and have mingled with the relatively small crowd of our quaint gathering. Their conversations, and the conversations of others, flourish and grow in volume and complexity as each new family member arrives. As we sit around discussing everything from my daughter's new computer to how madmen in the Mideast should be kept in check, our opinions differ as much as our outward appearances and individual personalities; and those differences are significant.

There is my wife's-cousin, Joyce, a self-prescribed environmentalist and latent hippie from the 1960's whose devotion to environmental causes and anti-capitalism ideologies are as solidly cast in stone as her variance from vegetarian meals whenever her, '*peers in just causes*', are not in view. Today's Thanksgiving dinner will qualify for such a digression from conviction.

Enters my brother-in-law, who is the president of an Oklahoma public television station. His livelihood, and 120,000 dollar paycheck, depends upon public funds. Oh boy, another liberal, tax-and-spend socialist in our midst. Add to this, two retired school teachers on union-derived pensions, a high-school guidance counselor, one retired college professor on pension benefits, a U.S. postal employee, and a retired military colonel on a government retirement pension and you'll conclude very quickly that my wife and I are outnumbered in our opinions against higher taxes. We are the only two in this room of ten paycheck earners, who don't derive our income from government funds.

"Know how much taxes were in 1913?" James Dee, the retired professor asks a few of our group in conversation.

James has his doctorate degree in Statistics with a minor in History from Michigan State University, so I figure he will know. But this subject of 'taxation' is taboo with our group, since tempers between me and everyone else usually begin to flare with the mention of the word. You see, in my opinion I am poor because people, like the government paycheck earners in this room, take my money. It isn't that I don't believe their jobs are valuable, it is just that as 'my employees', why do so many earn more than I do, working fewer hours? If I'm their employer, (which I am), then why don't I pay market wages? Extortion is the reason. And the extorters are called 'the government employee unions'. If the free market rule applied, we could hire the work much less expensively without losing quality. But I digress.

"Yes, I know all too well how much the taxes were in 1913!" was my response to James' inquiry. "But I'll bet my figures are higher than yours," I retort as my daughter and a few others leave the room knowing full well the ensuing conversation will not be worth bearing on an otherwise enjoyable Thanksgiving day.

"Well," said James, "the Federal tax rate was only one

percent of the average U.S. taxpayer's income, and the New York State income tax rate was only four percent of the average New York Sate taxpayer's earnings, making the total income tax a mere five percent."

"And how much is it today?" I asked, projecting a tone of dissention that sends an unconscious grimace into James' otherwise tranquil demeanor.

"Today's New York State Income Tax rate is eight percent and the Federal Tax rate is twenty-seven percent of the average taxpayer's earnings totaling thirty-five percent," he answers.

"No!" --With emotional charge, I begin my customary frustrating and aggravated rampage. "This is what exasperates me about the government. It's amazing that most people, like you, are not aware of their true tax rate. The New York State tax rate is not a simple eight percent. To that, add the darn Durham County sales tax of eight percent, the average property tax of 2.6 percent, sewer and water at point eight percent, fire at point one percent, and ...and...and...." As I begin to stutter and get frustrated, I pull a folded piece of paper from my wallet. Its age is shown by the many wrinkles and wear spots. As I aggressively unfold it, Jacob Whitten, the public television president, walks over to see what I have and quickly views the following data as I begin to pass the wrinkled sheet of numbers to James for his observation:

Tax	Percent of income (based on my joint family income of $80,000 per year)
Payroll Income Taxes:	
New York State	8.5%
Federal	27%
Social Security	6.3%
Medicare Tax	1.5%
Durham County Sales Tax:	8%
Property Tax:	
County	.5%
Town	.5%
School	1.5%
Fire	.1%
Sewer Tax:	.4%
Water Tax:	.4%
My Licenses:	
Hunting, Small Game	
Hunting, Large Game	
Trapping	
Fishing	
Pistol Permit	
Dog Licenses (2)	
Motor Vehicle Reg. (2)	
Driver's Licenses (2)	
Dump/Landfill use fee	1.6%

Hidden Taxes & Surcharges: NYS Hotel/Motel Surcharge Tax NYS Telephone Surcharge Tax NYS Liquor Surcharge Tax NYS Auto Fuel Surcharge Tax NYS Home Heating Fuel Surchg NYS Elec. Use Surcharge Tax	2%
Thruway, Bridge Toll, & Parking Taxes:	.1%
NYS Lottery User Fees (Tax) x 2:	.1%
NYS Health Expense Surcharge Tax charged by all emergency rooms and doctor's offices as reflected here as a pecent of gross annual income:	.6%

TOTAL TAXES PAID TO THE GOVERNMENT, BY MY FAMILY, IN 1997: 59.1%

Note: This table does not include inheritance taxes, capital gains taxes from the sale of a house, cigarette taxes, or any luxury item surcharge taxes that would serve to increase the total tax above the 59.1% tax rate. The many other taxes that affect New York State residents (like snowmobile or boat registrations) are not reflected in the above numbers since they do not currently impact my family. The above is simply a representation of my family's total annual tax rate.

I extend my arm out to James and hand him the income tax summary sheet as I begin my verbal assault against his prior blunder.

"Thi..i.. i..s is what we pay," I stutter. "Look at this! --It's out of control! It's outrageous that educated people, like you, actually feel that our New York State income tax rate is only eight percent. This is all government double speak as discussed and predicted in George Orwell's book, entitled "*1984*". The New York State government does not want us to know the combined total tax, so they hide the outrageous total amount by subdividing it into smaller governmental bureaucratic agencies, or as George Orwell would call them, *"Ministries"*. The amazing thing is that they get away with it. If everyone in America knew what they collectively paid in taxes, they would revolt. To avoid this, the government hides the total in smaller increments that seem easier to swallow.

"We Americans are fools," I stammer. "With such a gullible and unknowledgeable flock, it is no wonder our government leaders are able to convince us that taxes are good, people benefit, and taxes are necessary. James, you are a very knowledgeable individual, yet even you were convinced that our taxes were at lower levels until I showed you my paper."

My wife's sister, Joyce, sashays over with a drink in her hand as I continue.

"I am astonished that the United States Government is able to mislead us into thinking that our taxes are under their true fifty-nine percent mark," I add. "We are being misled like the animals in George Orwell's famous novel entitled, *"Animal Farm"*, and I think we will someday wake up to their fate. We will someday realize that while our leaders argue that they *'feel our pain'*, they are actually simply convincing us to work for them while they live *'the good life'*. They are actually using psychology at its finest to convince us to work for them, while they and their families prosper and enjoy a more comfortable life than ours. While we work like dogs 'till our death, they simply suck up our wages through taxes and spend the money on themselves and their own causes. They are actually manipulating those in the private sector to work sixty-hour weeks in order to pay for their genteel lifestyle and many causes, while their forty-hour weeks are spent convincing us that their cause is just." "Yes," I elaborate, "our government leaders spend their entire lives convincing us that the exorbitant taxes we pay and the lives spent for their benefit, in both work and in war, are for a good cause, while they are the greatest benefactors."

My rambling continues while the people gather around and listen, knowing not to interrupt due to the intensity of my ranting.

"The most significant expense in our lives are taxes," I continue. "All combined, my wife and I are forced to give over fifty-nine percent of our hard-earned income to the government. With this being the most significant factor in my family's spendable earnings, you would think the newspapers would print this number in the paper. For instance, a chart should show up in each Sunday edition showing the tax rate by year."

I slap another paper from my wallet down onto the table in front of James, and those in the group circle in their preparation to verbally lynch me at any second. (Sample of this paper follows):

Median State and Federal Combined Tax Rates
(Comparison by Year)

	1913	1927	1945	1950	1960	1970	1980	1990	**This Yr.**
State	4%	5%	9%	13.5%	14.8%	18.6%	19.2%	21.9%	**24.3%**
Federal	1.0	1.13	23	17.4	20.0	14.0	23.0	25.0	**27.0**
Other	n/a	n/a	1.3	2.2	4.1	5.2	6.0	6.8	**7.8**
Total	5%	6.13%	33.3%	33.1%	38.9%	37.8%	48.2%	53.7%	**59.1%**

Note:

1. *The State rate includes State Income Tax, Property Taxes, Licenses, and Fees.*
2. *The Federal tax rate represents income tax only.*
3. *'Other' represents Social Security and Medicare mandated payroll taxes (combined).*

"The newspapers list the stock rates, the bond rates, the rate of inflation, and the unemployment rate," I continue, "but why don't they list the single-most important index of all, --the tax rate? Why wouldn't they list this number that effects everyone and effects us all in a very signifi...." -- My ranting is finally interrupted by Joyce (as usual).

"Well, don't you think you should pay for caring for the poor or elderly?" says Joyce. "I suppose you wouldn't mind if the elderly had no medication or eyeglasses. You, who are politically seated to the right of Attila the Hun, wouldn't mind seeing children starve in America so that your family would not have to pay as much in taxes."

"What!" I exclaim. "What a bunch of unsubstantiated hype. There are plenty of wasteful programs that can be cut without hurting the poor or the elderly, and with the food stamp program already in place, I defy you to show me children starving to death in America due to lack of accessible food. This is the argument most used by tax and spend liberals like yourself, but with government food stamps, the school lunch program, and charity food pantries, there is obviously no substance to it. And now I suspect you'll use the typical liberal backup rhetoric that I am *'mean spirited'*, or something as vague an argument as that, to avoid answering my claim.

"What government programs would you cut?" demands Joyce.

"I would cut government employees' pay, to the same rate of earnings as those working in the private sector, in similar jobs. The reason for the government's growth from thirty-five percent of the U.S. work force to its current rate of fifty-three percent in the last twenty years is the attractiveness of the wage and benefit programs offered. They are so appealing that the government sector is attracting employees from the private sector like a high-powered magnet, thereby sending its total employment payroll to unaffordable levels."

"Take Colonel Whitney here," I say as I put my arm around Col. Richard (Dick) Whitney. "He retired from the military at the age of forty and has been earning twenty-five thousand dollars per year for the last fifteen years for doing NOTHING. Indirectly I am his boss, but I couldn't retire at age forty, so why did I let him?"

"Lets move over to Alan here," I say as I move to my wife's step-father's son who retired from a U.S. Post Office job at age fifty-five. "He receives twenty-five thousand dollars a year for doing NOTHING. Indirectly I am his boss, but I can't retire at the age of fifty-five, so why am I letting him?" He laughs and toasts glasses with his brother Jacob, who I verbally lynch next.

"And now we have Jacob Whitten. As president of an Oklahoma public television station he is paid 125,000 dollars per year. No wonder they are non-profit. *(A loud laugh resounds from the group in unison).* That rate would be fine if twenty percent of his station's revenues were not derived from government donations *(taxes).* I don't earn 125,000 dollars per year, and indirectly I am partially your boss. Why am I paying you so much when I can't afford it?" I exclaim as I pat him on the shoulder while he continues to chuckle and shake his head in a manner which serves to denote that nothing is going to change and that he enjoys being the beneficiary of this type of lofty pay, despite my complaints.

"James," I say affectionately, as I move from Jacob to him. "I think the world of you, but how did you get to retire from your professorship at Durham State Teacher's College at the age of fifty, pray tell? Now, I and my fellow taxpayers fund your retirement, paying a lofty forty-thousand dollars per year. I am indirectly your boss, and I can't retire at the age of fifty. Why can you?" I vociferate.

"Now for my last victim in the room," I say as I turn back towards Joyce and slowly walk toward her while springing my summary reprimand. "I indirectly pay you thirty-five thousand dollars per year to teach second grade children how to read and write. After only three years of being a teacher, you have already earned tenure so you're now guaranteed this position regardless of your performance or dedication. While I will concede that you are dedicated, I must launch two grievances on my former point."

"One, tenure should be earned after a period of ten years not three, but your teacher's union has perverted this age-old system of seniority in your favor. Tenure protection can now be achieved by teachers after only three years of employment."

"My second objection is your pay rate. After only three years of teaching, you earn thirty-five thousand dollars. Well, women *(in this geographic area)* with your experience and educational background, in the private sector, only earn between eighteen and twenty-eight thousand per annum and they don't have summers and school holidays off. They also usually lack the health benefits you enjoy but, ironically, they're the ones paying you for yours."

"I am worth that amount of money," she snaps.

"You're worth thirty-five thousand dollars for teaching eight-year-olds from a prepared text for less than a nine month period?" I retaliate. With school holidays, summer vacation, snow-days, and legal holidays you only work seventy-one percent of a year, but receive a paycheck based on a full-year of work. "If opened to the free-market system, you would be replaced by an employee who could do the same quality of work for much less pay. You would then be available for promotion within the system, to a position worthy of your desired salary. Instead, you vegetate as a second grade teacher since there is no monetary incentive to struggle for more. You're confident, I'm sure, that with guaranteed annual raises your pay rate will increase to a whopping forty-five thousand dollars a year when you reach fifty-years of age, therefore why change positions or strive for more?" --Especially when you only actually work seventy-one percent of a year.

"It is these kinds of disproportionally high wage and benefit packages that have attracted the masses to government positions and, as the pool of self-supporting government bureaucrats grows, it preys upon less fortunate souls like me who cannot afford its existence," I conclude. I am indirectly your employer, and I believe that paying thirty-five thousand dollars to teach second graders, for only seventy-one percent of a year, is too high a price to pay. I know of many unemployed and qualified teachers in the area willing to take the job for a fraction of your fee."

Joyce begins to act like there are tears in her eyes.

"Oh brother!" I thought. "Whenever their arguments fail from a logical perspective, the female liberals resort to tears. --And in regard to this conversation, her ploy, whether derived from the conscience or the sub-conscience level being inconsequential, has worked yet once again."

The group disperses, the comforters ask Joyce what is wrong, and the conversation on this topic ceases. "Oh brother," I think, "what a world!"

"Steve, can you help us in the kitchen, please?"

My wife, knowing I have caused trouble again, calls me into the kitchen to help grandma with another bogus *'man's carpentry'* project. We all know it is simply her diplomatic way to get me to drop my unwanted assault on the topic of over-taxation in preference to more important diversions like putting a nail in the kitchen wall for hanging a pot holder.

With this group of government paycheck receivers, nothing will be accomplished for the rights of the individual here today. At this gathering I, and my partner 'anxiety', am the minority. Here in my loneliness I long for a companion and find none. So much for Thanksgiving, I think.

One hour later dinner is served, adversarial topics are put to rest for another time, and we begin to enjoy the fine companionship that emanates from neutral topics discussed over a wonderful family meal.

"So Kelly," how's school going?" asks Marsha Whitten, a high school guidance counselor earning forty-thousand dollars on taxpayers money. --Much more than the twenty-three thousand dollars my wife earns in the private sector, working greater hours, as an administrative assistant at an International Plastic Molding company.

"Great, thank you!" responds Kelly politely.

"She has a ninety-eight percent average," interrupts my wife in her congenial attempt to contribute to the conversation and urge its continuance.

"Who's this coming to our door?" interrupts grandma, as she starts to rise from the dinner table while squinting to see who it is from the dining room window.

"Oh, it's Judith!" exclaims Grandpa Ed. "Let her in."

As grandma runs to the door to let Judith in, I think great! --I know who Judith is, and my conviction to this knowledge is reinforced with my wife's evil glare. A glare designed to communicate; --do not make a scene!

Enters Judith Bucci, --the gym teacher, purple hair and all; whose newspaper article favoring increased school taxes infuriated the occupants at O'Loughlin's Service Station over a month ago. Judith's parents live next door to Gram and Gramp and I presume Judith is visiting them for Thanksgiving.

"I can't stay long," comments Judith, as she exuberantly bursts into our dining room. "I hate to bother you at Thanksgiving. But, as you know, the last resolution to increase school taxes was turned down. I was hoping . . ."

"Have a seat," interrupts Grandpa Ed.

"Oh, all right. But just for a minute."

As Judith seats herself into grandma's vacant chair at our table, grandma sits into her knitting chair in the near corner of the room to listen intently.

"Well, as I was saying, the last tax increase vote was turned down, as you know. I am now soliciting signatures for a new vote. With a signature petition of two-hundred names, the issue can be re-addressed in ninety days. Is there anyone here who would like to sign this petition?"

It is passed to Joyce. Joyce diligently reads the introductory paragraph, pulls out her pen, and of course, --signs it. I say 'of course' because not only is she a liberal who believes in big government, but she is a teacher at the same junior high school the increased tax funds are designed to help. The words *'help'* and *'tax increase'* translate to *'pay raise'* and *'greater benefits'* to Joyce.

"The nice thing," comments Judith, "is that eventually we will simply wear down the taxpayers through our diligence. We teachers plan to bring this issue up for a re-vote every ninety days. All we need is one voting period devoid of a strong turnout by the blue collar class and we win, as usual. Steve do you want to sign?"

As everyone holds their breath and their glares descend upon my person; I respond as discretely as I know how, rather than risk the burden of ruining a family Thanksgiving once and for all. I also must be cautious with Judith, since she is the teacher who will decide my daughter's grade in this year's gym class. My daughter currently carries a ninety-five percent cumulative average, and a poor grade from Judith could skew that cume down significantly. I have heard from other parents that Judith can be vindictive against children and parents who disagree with her. It is unfortunate that the grades of the child can be tainted by a teacher's opinion of the parent(s), but that is the reality of our situation at the moment.

"Judith," I carefully respond. "You receive a weekly paycheck from the Grifton Junior High School, correct?"

"Yes."

"Are income taxes taken out of that paycheck?"

"Yes they are," she responds graciously with a questioning demeanor.

"Do you know what percentage of your paycheck is taken for government causes like social security, the New York State income tax, socialized medicine (Medicare/ Medicaid) or for the Federal income tax?"

"No," responds Judith. "I am not sure of the exact percent, but what does it matter?"

"I'm leading up to something," I respond. "The total taxes you pay, per year, currently exceeds a whopping fifty-nine percent. --That's F-I-F-T-Y N-I-N-E percent!" I exclaim. "Now you're telling me that you don't mind increasing your taxes even more than this already overwhelming amount?"

"Absolutely not," she responds quickly and with tone of malice. "It all goes to the kids and they deserve the best education they can get."

"Judith, since this school tax increase would effect both your and my property tax amount, please allow me to be more specific in an earnest attempt to make my point. Do you know what percent your current property tax rate would increase by this additional school tax levy of thirty-eight million dollars? Or do you simply pay in conjunction with your mortgage escrow payment, like many taxpayers, so that you are unaware of the specific rate amount?"

The group at our table is enraged with me. All eyes are on me. All faces are redder than usual. Grandma is up from her chair and on her way to the kitchen, and my daughter is making faces at me to cease this line of questioning.

Judith responds. "I don't pay property *(school)* taxes, since I live in an apartment in Durham."

My attempts for professional diplomacy are immediately flung aside as I verbally jump on this statement with rage.

-- "**THEN WHY SHOULD YOU HAVE ANY SAY IN HOW MUCH, THOSE OF US WHO ARE AFFECTED, WILL PAY?!**" I bellow.

"I am a teacher in that school sir, and I expect the best for my kids," counters Judith in an agitated state. "As an employee at Grifton Junior High School, I am entitled to vote on a school issue that effects me."

"Even though those issues cost others money, but cost you nothing because you live in an apartment outside of our school district?" I retort. "No," I exclaim as grandma re-enters the room. "I will not sign your . . ." I am interrupted again. "You are welcome to join us for dessert," Grandma tells Judith, in one of her many well-rehearsed ways of ending family disputes.

"No, thank you. I am leaving now," responds Judith.

"Please come back another time when we're not so busy," states grandpa.

"I will," retorts Judith.

"And bring your survey then," adds Marsha with a guidance counselor glare at me.

"Oh, I will," was Judith's response on her way out the door.

'Oh, I will,' echoed in my ears while the group once again verbally chastised me.

"Oh boy," I once again thought, "I am surrounded by the enemy and I can't even think of retaliation. --Oh brother, what a Thanksgiving!"

"When you are forced to work for the state, by the state, the state you're in is communism. While opportunities for happiness are stripped away by a burdensome collective tax rate, only the eagle can fly to safety while vulturous dictators encircle the brainwashed and the downtrodden masses."

Andrew Henry's diary dated the evening of November 26, 1998.

Chapter Three: The Drive Home

On the drive home from 'Grandma's' house, I couldn't help but to re-address my earlier arguments and since my wife and daughter were locked into my rapidly moving vehicle, they had no choice but to listen. Fortunately, my wife is sympathetic to my complaints.

"I don't believe Joyce pulled that, 'I lost the argument so now I'll cry for sympathy', routine again today."

"She always pulls that act when she loses her weak arguments based on emotion to stronger arguments based upon reason," answered my wife sympathetically.

"It's also a part of her calculated diversionary tactic to avoid the issues and still win arguments."

"You're right Andrew, but you know better than to bring up the subject of government spending and taxes with my family. As past and current government employees, they live off government paychecks. Do you ever think that they would agree with you that their checks are too large? They'll always want more money from the government, and they will always rationalize the amounts they receive no matter how out of step they are in relation to the general public."

"Well, I had mentioned to the group how we could save money by getting government paychecks and benefit programs in line with those of the private sector. And I addressed the fact that government employees should not be able to retire earlier than private-sector employees. But there are many other ways we can also save money, and reduce taxes, that I didn't have a chance to address."

"Look out for the deer."

"I see it." I responded to my wife as I slowed the car to a stop, in the fog. As the deer crossed in front of us, I continued my dissertation. "Other ways to reduce our tax burdens, include significantly reducing the money we now send overseas. I don't believe that our U.S. Foreign Affairs office gave away about 1,076 million dollars[1] to other counties to help them with their various problems and disasters." As the deer finally leaped into the safety of the roadside thickets, I accelerated and continued my monologue. "The money we spend on our foreign military bases makes sense, but augmenting a foreign government's tax revenues with U.S. tax receipts is idiotic and unfair. Number one, we don't have the money to spend since our national debt is over five trillion dollars with interest payments of about 242 billion dollars per year.[2] And number two, no other country gives us money to help with our problems or disasters, so why are we such suckers? These other countries must be laughing at our gullibility."

"Or they are just raking in our money graciously, figuring that if we're stupid enough to hand it out, they might as well take it," says Carol. "While our national debt climbs at a rate of an additional 523 million dollars per day, we keep handing it out to others. Why aren't we asking these other countries to hand money to us? We need it too!"

---

[1] *The Budget for Fiscal Year 1998*, p. 262.

[2] *Ibid*., p. 249.

"We can't afford to re-roof our house," I continue, "because it will cost five thousand dollars more than we have. I can't get a loan to roof it, since our credit is so bad. But the government can take 47,280 dollars of our personal income, via their 59.1 percent collective tax rate, and send a chunk of overseas. We even sent money to Russia this year *(200 million directly from the U.S. and 4.8 billion from the International Monetary Fund[3])*. Now Russia has enough money to build a nuclear weapons arsenal and send astronauts to space, but it needs our money for its communistic programs. I can't afford to fix my roof, but I can fund socialistic programs throughout the world? --No way!

As other examples of government waste, we gave Egypt 815 million dollars and Israel received five billion dollars this year. Why are average-income and poor American citizens giving them our money when we need it for our own families? I'm all for humanitarian aid, but most foreign aid is political in nature and unnecessary. Our current national debt load of 5.1 trillion dollars dictates that we can't afford philanthropy in other countries. If we have to pay foreign government officials to be friendly towards us, they are not true freinds; nor will they ever be. --I challenge them to send us money, and if they do, perhaps then my steadfast negative opinion would change.

The effects of our foreign funding escapades hurt our society in many ways. For example our county sewage treatment plant is polluting the river its effluent is pumped into, but rather than fix the problem by spending our tax dollars locally, we send money to foreign countries to dig wells and treat their sewage. How 'bout fixing our own problems before we take on the world? Good game fish like trout and bass can't survive downstream from our

---

[3] Russia Foreign Aid 1998., various internet sites.

sewage plant any longer, but we can clean the water in other counties. --How stupid. We can't drink the water from our own streams, but we've got the time and money to help clean up streams in other countries."

"That's nothing," chimed in Carol. "The President and his wife will be using Air Force Two to fly to New York City this weekend for a Democratic fund-raising dinner. The pre-sold tickets generated five-hundred thousand dollars in revenue, but the plane will cost the taxpayers thirty-five thousand dollars per hour to fly. It is an hour flight from Washington to the Newark Airport, so let's figure an hour both ways. That's seventy thousand dollars in plane fares alone before you add limo service, the helicopter escorts, meals, hotel rooms, local police escort, secret service escort, entertainment expenses, etc."

"How do you come up with thirty-five thousand dollars an hour for the plane?"

"Remember, I visited the Wright-Patterson Air Force Base public museum last year when Mom and I took our trip out to Dayton to visit my brother in the hospital. While Chad was recovering from his back surgery, Mom and I stopped one afternoon at the United States Air Force Museum. While we were there, we had the chance to see the current Air Force Two presidential plane up close. That thing was the largest plane I've ever seen in my life. I was in such awe of its size, that I had to ask the museum curator how much it cost us taxpayers. He told me the astonishing amount of thirty-five thousand dollars an hour and, by looking at the plane's size, I could believe it.

He added that the original price was over 120 million dollars and it holds 57,285 gallons of jet fuel.[4] At the current cost of seventy cents per gallon, that's 40,100 dollars in fuel alone. And since fifteen to twenty-five percent of an

---

[4] Jet Fuel, Internet, 1998.
Boeing 747, Internet, 1998.

airplane's operating cost is jet fuel, the total operating cost of thirty-five thousand dollars per hour is a realistic estimate of Air Force Two's operating costs. Especially when you include depreciation and maintenance costs.

It has an upper and lower deck and can carry ninety-three people. It could fit 450 passengers if it were used as a traditional Boeing 747 double-wide/double-deck airliner, but as the presidential plane, much of the room is taken up with tables, beds, sinks, work-desks, press rooms, and such."

"I'm sorry that I interrupted you to inquire how you came up with your costs. Please go on with your original story."

"My point is that this fund-raiser for the Democratic Committee will generate five-hundred thousand dollars at a cost to the taxpayer of seventy-thousand dollars in air fare alone. Now why isn't the taxpayer reimbursed for the use of Air Force Two when it is used to generate funds for private purposes?

The trip from Washington, D.C. to Newark, N. J. was a short one, but just think how many fund-raisers the President and/or his wife attend each year. I know they're scheduled in Cincinnati, Ohio for two Democratic fund-raising dinners next month."

"And one in Los Angeles in May," I added.

"Add them all up, and they're having a grand old time funding their causes at taxpayer expense."

"It's not just the Democrats who use public property as vehicles for funding private causes. When Republican presidents had occupied the White House, they used Air Force One to fly to Republican fund-raising dinners."

"I know," responded Carol. "But my point is that we are plagued with domestic spending wastes as well as foreign spending wastes. The government is on a loose purse string and its members and leaders are taking advantage of us all.

They're even helping fund business overseas, despite the fact that our own American based companies are closing their doors at record numbers. Just in our county alone, five substantial companies closed their doors this year because they couldn't compete with foreign imports. Get this, -- we have funded foreign economies through our Economic Support Fund and our Overseas Private Investment Corporation to the tune of 3,924 million dollars.[5] Why not simply fund our own U.S. economic business sector by not taking that money out of the taxpayer's pocket in the first place? Then, the money the taxpayer saves could be spent on domestic goods and services. Let's not take care of the world, until we can reduce our crippling tax burdens on U.S. citizens and get it down to a more affordable 39.1 percent collective tax rate. –Let's get some foreign countries to invest in America's financial well being, for a change, until we've paid off our own national debt load."

"I know," I responded to Carol, "but it doesn't do any good for either of us to continue complaining about it. And neither of us has time to fight the system since we're too busy working all day just make ends meet."

"Then stop complaining, Dad," quipped my daughter from the back seat, "and could you please turn on the radio?"

"No." I blurted out in anger.

"Kelly," scolded my wife, with a sympathetic tone in her voice. "Let your father vent or he'll make our lives miserable for the rest of the drive home."

"I may make your lives miserable, but our government makes my life miserable. By taking the money I need to fix our roof, we may not have a house soon. If water begins

---

[5] *The Federal Budget for Fiscal Year 1998*, p. 23.
OPIC (Overseas Private Investment Corporation), Internet site, 1998.
The Economic Support Fund, 1998., various internet sites.

leaking into your bedroom ceiling, and onto your bed, you'll quickly join me in my rantings. The old asphalt shingles over your bedroom are cracking with age and gradually blowing off our roof. Our roof's in ruins and I can't afford to fix it. My entire life has been ruined by a government that can't keep its hands out of my pockets. Do you know that I've got to come up with 2,080 dollars to pay our property taxes this month? --That was money we could have used to repair our roof, but I have to hand it over to our government, in addition to the nearly 45,200 dollars in taxes your mom and I have already paid this year."

"We know," responds my wife sympathetically, "but you're making your points to the wrong people."

"Well, I can't complain to the town hall. The government is closed in the evenings and on the weekends. I work during the day and can't spend my time lobbying government bureaucrats to reduce their spending or I'll be out of a job."

"That's right, Honey. We can never win, so just put up with it. Taxation and increased tax rates are a fact of life. The government's overwhelming pool of bureaucrats and legislators have all day to fight for their causes and we don't. You might as well just accept it."

"That's the problem with Americans. Most of us are too busy and tired to fight our oppressive government. The irony of that fact, is that our government's inaccessibility on evenings and weekends is what protects it from our wrath and inevitably allows it to grow uncontrolled."

"Dad," interrupts Kelly. "Please give up and turn on the radio. You're driving me crazy."

As my wife looks at me with her we'll rehearsed look denoting, 'give-the-kid-a-break', I allow the music to take over. The rest of the way home I mentally reflected on how there are hundreds and thousands of ways to reduce government spending. Every American citizen can think of dozens of ways based on his or her personal experiences. But those of us who work in the pseudo-capitalistic sector are forced to spend our 8 to 14 hour days working, as opposed to lobbying the government. You would think that those we elect would understand our economic plight and help us. But the financial wants of their position too often take precedence over the needs of the citizens they represent. And a collective tax rate of 59.1 percent, a national debt of over five trillion dollars, and a track record of legislators receiving inordinate pay raises validates my negative opinion of our government leaders.

This year our city mayor proposed a nineteen percent pay raise for himself from eighty-four thousand dollars to 100,135 dollars. Our state legislators boosted their pay by thirty-eight percent to 79,500 dollars this year, up from 57,500 dollars. The city schools superintendent got the board to vote for his annual salary to raise from 101,000 dollars to 123,000 dollars without voter approval. The median income of our area is twenty-nine thousand dollars per year. The typical pay raise in the private sector is 2 to 4%. How do these government officials feel that taxpayers in the private sector can afford their greed? The answers are simple: They will push for whatever they can get away with, until they are stopped by the voices of hundreds of disgruntled taxpayers.

"I have found, with age and wisdom, that there is a catch to most everything in life."

Andrew Henry's diary dated November 27, 1998.

Chapter Four: The Catch

As in Joseph Heller's novel entitled, Catch 22, I also have a catch in my life that keeps me somewhere between sanity and that unstable world that pulls all of us toward its outer limits on a daily basis. I will call it Catch A-23. In Heller's story, a combat pilot argues that it is crazy for him to fly more combat missions since, as the mission rate increases, so do his odds of death. Heller's Catch 22 stated that if the pilot was crazy, he would not have to fly any more missions. --But since he was sane enough to know he would be crazy to keep flying, then he wasn't actually crazy and would have to continue despite his objections. This twisted logic is similar to my Catch A-23 which states that while most people chose political careers to champion their particular cause, I am expected to pay for their cause through additional taxes levied against me, when I don't benefit. While I am expected and required, by law, to fund the dreams, ambitions, and desires of the community politicians, my catch A-23 disallows me to fund my own dreams, ambitions, and desires. Although that's the main catch, there is also another catch which I will call Catch J-24.

My Catch J-24 states that while everyone in society has a breaking point where his/her collective tax rate becomes objectionable, few will object until it is too late to reverse the decisions that got them to that point of objection. Rather, they will first grow to accept the tax, then rationalize its existence, and finally embrace it as a necessary part of their lives.

We are a people who are easily lead. Why complain against the voice of the masses, when to do so would alienate you from society? The Catch J-24 is that; --perhaps those in the masses feel like you do but, like you, are too timid to speak out.

" No one can be truly free, until they are free of debt."

Andrew Henry's diary dated December 7, 1998.

Chapter Five: Bankrupt

The North American Free Trade Agreement between our two bordering countries was not only a great idea for the U.S. consumer, but its full enactment this January of 1999 will open a new world of sales opportunities for me in Canada. Since New York State borders the major access routes to both Toronto and Montreal, I have begun canvassing those two metropolitan cities with a renewed zest for life.

Finally, I think, I may become wealthy with the quick additional sales that I will be able to secure in Canada due to the enactment of this agreement between our two countries. At last, I can free myself from a sea of relentless creditors who have, up to this point, kept me from rising further than my current, oppressed, station in life. With renewed energy and enthusiasm I phone my boss at NPM Paper Company to ensure that my efforts in Canada will be adequately rewarded. My first question to Mr. Finestine is:

"Are there any limitations to the commission dollars that I can earn, now that we will be adding Canada to my sales territory?"

A pause and then a resounding, "No limitations!" emanated from the phone receiver into my anxious ear. This response was exactly what I had hoped to hear and, since Mr. Finestine was a member of the ownership of this family run company, I had no reason to request a collaborating answer from any others at NPM Paper. Wanting to be sure of my position, however, I next cited a specific example to further clarify my parameters.

"Mr. Finestine," I enthusiastically began, "you are telling me that if I make two-hundred thousand commission dollars from working diligently, NPM will not cut my commission rate back, fearing that I am making too much money for a mere salesman?"

"Nope!" was again the reply that I had hoped to hear.

"Mr. Finestine," I concluded, "you mean that I could even make a million dollars and the accountants, managers, and other owners at NPM would not become envious and then cut back my commissions?"

Again, a collaborating, "Nope!"

"Wherever you sell our product," he added, "whether it be in your current territory of New York State, or your upcoming territory of Canada, we will support you by honoring your current commission structure ON ALL SALES!"

During the next five minutes of routine conversation, all I could hear in my head were Mr. Finestine's prior words of 'COMMISSION ON ALL SALES!' echoing within my mind. I jotted the words down on my note pad while his monologue continued on the phone. My mind wandered as I imagined how I would tell my wife this encouraging news when she arrived home this evening. I dreamt about how I would spend the extra money I would earn this year. It could be spent on fixing our roof, which was in desperate need of new asphaltic shingles. The money could be spent on painting our house, or perhaps I could take my wife and daughter for a weekend trip to New York City. Or perhaps just pay off our many bi . . . "Well, I'll talk to you again tomorrow, Andrew."

The following silence on the line woke me instantaneously from my daydreaming back to an embarrassing reality.

As I haphazardly regained my bearing, I responded, "Yea! . . Yes, Mr. Finestine, I will talk to you tomorrow."

"Good luck to you in Canada my boy," were his final words before the sound of the dial tone completely brought me back into focus from my daydreaming.

As I glared out the window of my upstairs office, the world in view looked wonderful. With my mind now full of ideas, and my body full of renewed ambition, I immediately began my plans for an upcoming trip to Toronto.

One year from the date of my first Toronto sales call I had acquired eight new truckload accounts. All of these accounts were obtained in Canada, and my family and I were prospering from my extra commission dollars. We never did fix the roof or paint the house. We simply splurged on the many impractical things that we had always longed for. Energized by my first year's successes in Toronto and later in Montreal, I spent the following year going after business in other Canadian towns. In the Province of Ontario, accounts located in St. Catharines, Hamilton, Mississauga, Kitchener, and London were added to my active customer list. To my Quebec Province business, I quickly added accounts from the suburbs of Montreal and then gradually worked my way up Route 40 to obtain business in TroisRivie'res, Quebec City, and eventually towns as far to the north as Ragueneau. My sales were now increasing at a rate of thirty percent per year, and the extra commission dollars were generously spent prospecting for more Canadian business. My American Express credit card balance had hit its maximum level of ten thousand dollars when I was sabotaged by my Canadian competitors and my own company, simultaneously, without warning.

The Canadian manufacturers are government subsidized; therefore, U.S. companies can not truly compete against them effectively. After I had eroded their sales to an irritable level, my Canadian competitors not only fought back, -- they fought back with a vengeance. When I had arrived in Canada two years prior, my prices were twenty percent lower than the Canadian prices. This year, my prices suddenly changed to being ten percent higher than Canadian prices. The Canadian paper companies, who had now experienced enough of my market disruption, collectively decided that there would be no more U.S. intrusion. My newly acquired Canadian customers dropped me for the more favorable Canadian prices, while my own company gave up on this market, since they could no longer be competitive. To make matters worse, NPM was increasing its pricing in an attempt to diminish excess demand in a few prosperous U.S. territories and maximize profits. Unfortunately for me, the price increase was universal. When NPM management announced the five percent increase, it was to be instituted in all sales territories, including my already wavering Canadian territory.

"Why are you increasing my prices in Canada, while my business up here is already in decline?" I asked Kurt Henderson one night in desperation. Kurt was president of Trade Relations for NPM, and I was calling him at his Connecticut residence from a pay phone in the lobby of the plush Hotel DeVille', located in a prosperous area of northern Montreal. It was a Friday evening at 6:45 P.M. and I was exhausted, disgusted, depressed, and mildly inebriated after spending forty-five minutes in the hotel lounge, mentally reviewing my predicament. "Why isn't NPM supporting me?" I asked Kurt. "Prices keep going down in Canada, while NPM's prices keep going up. --I'm getting killed out here."

Kurt responded, in his usual caring way, by asking for specific details and then stating that he would bring up my plight at NPM's Monday morning management meeting. Our discussion was short, since he knew that I was disgusted. Kurt and I had voiced this same conversation for the past three months and, I now realize, nothing will be done. Kurt is simply too much of an optimist and diplomat to tell me straight-out that NPM Paper had given up on that market, but I now see all too painfully the picture that has been dramatically painted for me by my employer and my competitors. --I am done in Canada!

I hang up the phone, I return to my table, and I stare at the wall while my third Manhattan glass sits empty on the table before me. As my body remains frozen in a state of zombie-like-shock, my mind reels with questions emanating from the two years that I have diligently worked this Canadian market.

"After all my work, why isn't NPM responding aggressively to retain business here? --Why are they letting me lose one account after another without even making an attempt to retaliate? --Why did I spend so much money trying to develop this market? --Brother, what a fool I am!" I mumble to myself.

My mind had been blinded by greed, and for that error I shall now suffer the pains of a maimed spirit for eternity and, unbeknownst to me at this time, my wife and daughter would suffer a lifetime in the wake of my ensuing rage. My sales days in Canada are now finished, and it is time to sober up for the drive back to my New York State residence.

"It is also time," I mumble to myself as I rise from the table, "to look for another job."

As I stood and began walking to the dining room, the physical pains from a life of work now pushed their way back into the forefront of my psyche, as is typical during my bouts with depression. I was lethargic, and my mind reeled with the memories of my pleasant, then painful, rise and fall from grace in Canada as I walked to the dining room in a daze. After my meal and two cups of coffee, I began what I knew would be my last drive home from Canada. Departing at 9:00 P.M., I would miss the heavy Montreal commuter traffic and would arrive at my New York State residence at approximately 4:00 A.M. During the drive, I rationally thought about my plight, and what my colleague Chas Gallo had once told me three years ago during one of my bragging episodes. Chas's advise was to pay closer attention to NPM's operating capacity and less time bragging about my increased sales levels. At the time, I suspected Chas was simply jealous of my sales successes. Chas was an eighteen-year sales veteran at NPM, and I now realize that his recommendations were heartfelt realities based on experience. --I had simply been an arrogant fool not to believe his earnest words of advice. Chas had told me that when NPM is operating at ninety percent of capacity, they are willing to make price concessions. The problem, he said, was that if the salesmen go out and increase our business significantly, NPM would raise prices to avoid inventory stock-outs. When I later questioned my sales manager about that concept, he had promised that, 'growth at NPM Paper Company would be welcomed'. "As we obtain more business," he had stated, "NPM would relish the opportunity to add additional production equipment and facilities designed to keep ahead of strong demand." I erroneously chose to believe my boss, rather than my colleague, and I now see all too clearly the predicament in which I have placed my fellow salesmen and myself. My sales increases of thirty percent, accompanied with NPM's over all growth, has spurred production levels to a rate of ninety eight percent of capacity. I see clearly now that NPM does not mind losing low-price business in Canada or low margin U.S. sales territories, since participation in that business would jeopardize business in their more profitable U.S. markets. If NPM had lowered their prices to keep my Canadian accounts active, sales demands would have exceeded the company's production capabilities. Since the residents of this now densely populated area of central Connecticut would disallow plant expansion, NPM opted to simply let their unprofitable Canadian business disappear while focusing on servicing sales in their more profitable U.S. markets. NPM's plan was a natural progression, but I was too ignorant to see it coming. Out of greed I had erroneously chosen to believe my boss, rather than face reality and I am now paying a heavy price for my folly. Even though my sales days are through in Canada, the managers at NPM still abstain from admitting to it. They would rather have me spend money attempting to generate profitable business in Canada than recommend that I give up and lose any available profitable opportunities in that country. The problem is that, if I continue to work Canada, my cost of sales will significantly exceed any commission earnings generated. I am already burdened with an increased debt load of ten-thousand dollars since I had erroneously chosen to believe that this investment in the Canadian territory would have allowed me to build my business to an extremely rewarding level. I was wrong, and Chas Gallo was correct. --There is only so much product NPM can produce, and that product will only be sold to those distributors willing to pay the highest price. I have been intentionally misled by my company, but only have myself to blame. In my overwhelming desire to break away from my austere world, I had run to the light of greed. It was only that light that I wanted to see. No one's words, no one's rationale, no one's opinions would turn my head from that light, --that ray of hope. I do not regret having tried and failed at the attempt. Rather, my regret stems from the fact that I was betrayed by those managers who knew of my eventual plight and offered no warning of its eventuality. Their greed outweighed their compassion, and their successes and promotions at the company will be earned from the failures of unsuspecting pawns like me.

For the next year I struggled with my business in New York State. Having increased my credit card debt load by ten thousand dollars while in Canada, I could never recover. My family and I went bankrupt by year's-end. Our opinions of one another are now compromised, the mention of divorce follows arguments much too frequently, and our opportunities have been further diminished by our now poorer credit rating. These increased obstacles in our life have taken their toll on my New York State sales as well. I am now losing business at a rate of 10 percent per year. Most of this loss comes from the fact that I lack the funds to visit my customers as often as needed. But, I have learned from my negative Canadian experience that you must establish a budget, and stick to it, no matter how overwhelming the desire to chase your dreams. There is only so much product a company can produce, and an extremely sensitive balance exists between cost of sales, sales volumes, and production capacity. Unfortunately this reality has turned me into more of a realist, more of a pessimist, and less of a salesman!

Upon arriving home at 4:00 A.M. and falling into a sound sleep in my bed, I dreamt the following dream: As I descended through dark and pillowy clouds in the sky, my first vision of earth was the outlining borders of the state of Connecticut. Next, I was floating above the NPM paper plant located in McCormick, Connecticut. I was hovering over the plant while looking down at its brick and metal structure. From four towering stacks, a light-gray smoke plumed into the air, while a dark reddish-brown sludge could be seen entering the Flintwell River running just behind the plant. Suddenly, from its dormancy, the head and neck of what appeared to be a huge, menacing monster rose up from the roof of the building and swayed in the sky as it towered over the plant. Although dinosaur-like in appearance, the monster did not seem threatening. The manufacturing plant's appearance had turned into a living, breathing, monster that resembled the extinct Tyrannosaurus Rex of the Jurassic period. It seemed more mechanical in motion, however, as its breastplate of iron, scales of brick and metal, and four spiked horns of an unknown composition all glistened with its motion. Its feet of mortar and stone did not move, and thankfully so, for had they moved the slightest millimeter they would have encroached on the land and dwellings of the many residential properties that had sprung up over the years to now surround it. As my body floated to face this monster's fire red eyes, I could see in them, a state of self-pity. There was nothing for me to fear. There was only a sad and slowly dying monster looking at me as if it knew that I could understand its plight. We both felt comfort in our silent communion while a human voice could be heard narrating in a monotone that emanated from nowhere or everywhere, I could not discern.

The monster's heart beat loud and firm, like the deep, rich sound of a hundred kettle drums, and then the words from the voice rang clear to my ears.

"Like the dinosaurs of days past, this dinosaur of the industrial age will die at last." Another heartbeat pound interrupts the narrator, and then he begins again.

"Though armed with a breastplate of steel and scales of brick and lead, this dinosaur too will soon be extinct and dead."

The monster now moves its head and looks at me with the pathetic glance that serves to communicate its knowledge of its impending and unfair demise.

"With its environment now taken away," the narrator continues, *"it will now be politicians' prey, and using their weapons of ordinances and codes for its destruction, they will regulate its life away."*

"A society embracing equality must treat its citizens impartially,or be despised as bestowing prejudicial treatment towards or against it's individual members."

Andrew Henry's diary dated May, 2004.

Chapter Six: Prejudice

Three years and four months have elapsed since my bankruptcy and the post-industrial revolution giant called <u>NPM Paper Company</u> is surprisingly still running strong, although physical plant expansion shall henceforth remain a political and logistical impossibility at its now densely populated State of Connecticut location. Recently, a sales position was left vacant in NPM's Ohio sales territory with the resignation of my colleague, Paul Cummings. When Mr. Finestine asked if I would like to add that territory to my current New York State account base, I jumped at the opportunity. I needed the extra income to help me pay the many overdue bills that have attached themselves to my person like a legion of demons, refusing to relinquish their command of my being. Sure, I know that most would think me a fool to be back in the throes of a debt-infested world after receiving bankruptcy relief only three and a quarter years prior, but this procedure did not exorcise these many demons that haunt me. It only served to hold them at bay for a little while.

I still suffer from an onslaught of expenses, taxes, and debts that riddle me with pain to a point that death seems to be the only way of escape. But it must be a natural death, since my religious convictions forbid suicide. As a Catholic, suicide is **not** viewed as an acceptable escape from the miseries of temporal life into the hands of a loving

God. It is viewed as a transgression against God, punishable by eternal damnation in a metaphysical pit of demons so demented and punishing that nothing exists but eternal misery for the souls that are lost to this fiery realm.

Other options of escape are also blocked. I cannot work greater hours, since I am already working fourteen hours a day for NPM with additional hours spent maintaining my decrepit house in New York State. I cannot pay off my creditors, since I lack the funds. I cannot obtain a better paying job, since my pay rate is already at the top of the stratum for professionals with my educational background. And I cannot sell my house, since its debt load exceeds its value.

I not only pity myself with this agonizing paradox I am forced to face, but I pity a world of people in the same contemptible position as me. We work and get nowhere and the pain is intolerable in the face of the bleak future we will be held to by a government that feels that collecting a greater portion of our income than the portion we receive is absolutely justifiable. The distribution of wealth and power in America is inherently set against any individual who embarks on his/her life without the blessings of family money to help them begin their journey. I started with nothing, and the mammoth wave of tax collectors and bill collectors has risen against me to ensure my subservience to their cause. When I started my career in sales, my American dream was to be proud, independent, and successful. --My government has helped to make this dream an intolerable nightmare with intrusive rules, regulations, and excessive taxes. I know by an American bankruptcy rate of ten percent, that I am not alone in my misery. Others who have been forced into this pitiable position, and tens of thousands more on the brink of this unfortunate realm, join me in my insufferable plight.

To find relief, I must take the job offered to me in Ohio. The task will be difficult and I will miss my family during my absence, but I have no choice but to take on that position to help keep my creditors and various tax collectors at bay. I cannot seek bankruptcy relief again for another seven years, nor do I want to resort to that humiliating and demoralizing event ever again. There is a risk that these additional sales responsibilities will turn into another financial nightmare like that experienced in Canada, but my creditors leave me no choice. I am cornered with nowhere to go but Ohio.

The following week, I despairingly loaded my autovan with my clothes, my computer, and various sales catalogues for my journey to the flat lands of Ohio. Upon arriving in Decorah, Ohio I found an efficiency apartment and moved in immediately. Two phone lines were installed (one for my fax machine and one for my business phone), and immediate preparations were made for visits to my many Ohio customers in an attempt to introduce myself and keep their business activities with NPM active.

During the first three months in Ohio, I was only able to visit my New York State customers and my family one week per month. I was extremely busy in Ohio, introducing myself to my many customers and their sales force and conducting sales meetings at their place of business. My life was moving at an extremely fast pace, and I lacked the time to observe the world around me until my fourth month in Decorah. It was then that I suddenly realized that something very special and peculiar was happening in the neighborhood in which I lived. I began to slowly notice that the black people in my neighborhood were ecumenically prosperous. They drove luxury cars, they worked on their well-maintained homes and yards with diligence, and they prospered at their varied careers without there being a sense of racial tension behind the scenes. It was wonderful to witness. When I first realized this phenomena taking place around me, I began to actively search for confirmation of my first observation. I drove to a local schoolyard shortly after the lunch hour to find black children, white children, Hispanic children, and Asian children all playing in their school yard integratedly, without the grouping together I was accustomed to in New York State. My barber was a black person, my lawyer was a black person, my doctor was an Indian from India, and my banker was a black person. From top to bottom, the City's residents seemed to be devoid of prejudice in favor of, or against, any race, creed, or color. It was wonderful to witness everyone in this small city of 53,226 people prosper in an environment that facilitated a life style based solely upon ones ambition and ability, as opposed to ones race. Doctors, lawyers, politicians, homemakers, ironworkers, barbers; everyone chose their life's work by desire and ability without an issue of race impacting their decisions. Every day I left my office apartment to sell in other areas of Ohio, I would drive by people of all nationalities and backgrounds working harmoniously on their homes and at their places of work in an earnest effort to build a better life for themselves and their families.

In my attempt to understand how this city had transformed to such a splendid example of racial harmony, I first visited the Decorah, Ohio Public Library. There, I found the first clear answer to my quandary in the *Ashwood County Census Report* dated *for the Year Ended 12-31-2003*. As can be discerned by the following example, it was completely devoid of prejudice towards any group of people. Only persons who were not citizens of the United States, or those who had only been citizens for a period of not more than one year, were able to denote their nationality. All others were grouped together as **'Americans'** as illustrated below:

2003 CPH-L-81. Selected Social Characteristics: 2003	
Table 1. Ashwood County, Ohio	
ANCESTRY	
Total ancestries reported	144,528
Arab	7
Austrian	4
Belgian	9
Canadian	0
Czech	1
Danish	7
Dutch	8
English	4
Finnish	3
French (except Basque)	8
French Canadian	4
German	3
Greek	6
Hungarian	4
Irish	0
Italian	6
Lithuanian	6
Norwegian	6
Polish	0
Portuguese	3
Romanian	7
Russian	5
Scotch-Irish	4
Scottish	4
Slovak	5
Sub-Saharan African	3
Other African	8
Swedish	9
Swiss	5
Ukrainian	2
United States or American	**144,370**
Welsh	1
West Indian (excluding Hispanic origin	4
groups)	9
Yugoslavian	3
Other ancestries	
Note: Ancestries are based on first generation birthright and citizenship United States Citizens residing in America for more than one year shall be listed as 'Americans'	

This is wonderful, I thought. Rather than set up walls of prejudice by defining racial divisions, the census bureau united its citizenry with the use of one word: 'AMERICANS'. Since it is unlawful to discriminate, why do we do so by labeling any American by a special label. Except for the American Indian, none of us are indigenous to America, so why provide special titles or treatment to any American immigrant, since to do so would serve only to establish racial divides, which then breed special treatment or prejudice toward or against various groups of people.

The effect of this revelation was so simple yet dynamically profound to my mental bearing, that I let out a gasp that immediately alerted the librarian to my person. As my eyes met hers, my first reaction was to walk towards her, apologize, and explain the wonderful reason for my outburst. Then a second revelation came to me. If I were to discuss this topic with the librarian, or investigate further, I would infringe on the very principals of this town's people that I so admire: --not only their lack of prejudice, but also their lack of discussion over matters of race, creed, or color since that would, in itself, foster discrimination. I elected to return my census papers to their shelves, immediately cease my research on the topic, and return to the City streets of Decorah, a vastly improved 'AMERICAN'.

"As a society grows, must we acquiesce to its needs by forfeiting our individuality?"

Andrew Henry's diary dated Nov. 17, 2004.

Chapter Seven: The Militia

As I stand alone on the west bank of the Ohio River, watching the slow-moving current drift south and meander its way west toward the heartland of America, the fall of the year has already brought darkness to my place in the world at this early evening hour of 6:00 P.M. While the moon's beams dance their eerie and haunting dance off the many ripples of the current before me, uneasy thoughts flow to me and from me, . . .--but from whom and to whom I can not discern. It is as if I am a standing receptor of thoughts from the cosmos, or perhaps they are simply thoughts from within my being. I would rather think the former, as I would earnestly like to be a part of a greater presence. I jump, as my horse pulls another leaf from a bush, and I then return to my mental contemplations as she chews in a relaxed-standing position to my rear. With her reigns in my right hand and my hunting rifle draped comfortably over my left forearm, I try to sort out these feelings that are haunting me on this cool and quiet November night. While I stare into the sparkling moon-lit current of the Ohio River flowing soothingly past, the thoughts flowing through me are not consistent in their presence, nor do they encompass feelings of warmth. They are rather; random thoughts, --sporadic thoughts; they are, . . .I suppose, ... lonely thoughts. I have companions tonight; --they wait for me only a half a kilometer up the hill where their campfire light silhouettes the lean-to we will be sleeping in tonight, --but I long for home.

"Come-on Sussie," I command the mare as we turn toward the camp and my companions who await our arrival. "Lets go!" With a gentle tug of the reigns we begin our eight-minute ascent up the dew-soaked field to the camp, meandering around scrub-brush thickets as we ascend.

"Hey Andrew, see anything?" was the greeting provided by John Cindrich upon entering the well-lit perimeter of the fire.

"Yea, there was a herd of large doe in the meadow 2.5 kilometers south of here, but I'll wait for my twelve point buck before I take a shot."

John and our other guest for the evening laugh in unison as I secure Sussie in her rustic outdoor pen with the two other horses.

"Boy it's nice up here," I mention to John as I turn from the horse pen and begin walking toward the campfire.

The seat left open for me by my two camping companions was the best seat in our camp. As I sat on the center edge of the open-ended lean-to, I faced out toward the campfire crackling only two meters in front of me. As I peered out over the fire's flames, I could view the great Ohio below, silhouetted by the neighboring trees, and flowing soothingly past with sparkles of moonlight reflecting off its many ripples. John was sitting on a large meter wide fire log set on end, two paces to my right, while Jim Fletcher was settled comfortably on a large, rounded rock slightly over one meter to my left. Illuminated by the fire, their facial characteristics were accentuated. John's face was very large, as it should be to fit his 6'4" tall, solidly constructed physique of 245 pounds. His eyes were surrounded by black framed glasses that seemed as if they were an outdated style from the 1950's, and his black hair was conservatively short and parted to the right in a common style for businessmen of our era. Jim's features to my left contrasted John's in every way. His was a gentler face, mounted on a smaller frame of only 175 pounds. He wore a mustache and possessed slightly receding, mousy blond hair, with gray streaks at the side burns. His soft spoken and non-aggressive demeanor served him well as a purchasing agent and warehouse foreman at John's company, but his soft speech was difficult for me to hear on this night with the wind rustling the leaves around us. As Jim spoke I would have to lean toward him to hear.

"Want some venison?"

"Sure!" I replied as Jim passed a plump venison steak using the hot frying pan that he had just removed from the grill positioned atop our campfire. As I quickly grabbed a nest-kit metal plate and passed it his way, he rotated the pan so the steak slid, --and then plopped into my plate.

"Thanks Jim," I replied.

"So you didn't see that buck yet Andrew?" interrupted John in his attempt, I presume, to make me feel welcomed and initiate conversation.

"Nope, but I saw a lot of beautiful country."

"Oh, yea!" John retorted. "Not only is this a beautiful area, but my family owns 275 acres of it. That's why we can ride these horses around without getting shot by other dear hunters. --It's posted property and nobody better be on this land but a Cindrich without permission."

"Well, the florescent-red horse blankets and the silly looking red horse hats don't hurt either," laughed Jim, as all of our laughter immediately accompanied his.

"Andrew," John began again, "later tonight my brother Daniel is going to be joining us and we all have something important to talk to you about. It has nothing to do with the paper business, but I think that you're the type of person who would be very interested in hearing our proposition."

"Sure," I replied with a questioning tone. John immediately returned his conversation to topics of hunting and camping thereby giving me the distinct impression that the proposition would be better addressed upon Dan's later arrival. The next two hours flew by with the swift elapse of time that usually accompanies engaging conversation. We had talked about our hunting, fishing, and trapping experiences and had just changed to the lofty topic of which brewery made the best beer when we were abruptly interrupted by a voice in the woods to my left.

"Don't shoot. --It's only the natives," was the voice's command.

John replied with a, "Get over here. We've saved a nice cold one for you."

I presumed that meant a beer rather than a cold venison steak and I further assumed that the voice was that of John's brother since John and Jim did not seem alarmed.

Dan entered our campsite with the exuberance of a lad twenty years younger. At forty years of age, he acted like an energetic twenty-year-old.

"Hi Andrew!"

Dan stretched out his right hand to shake mine. "How ya' doin'?" he asked with his breathing strained from his terrestrial trek to our site and with an excited and possibly nervous rambling that continued without waiting for my reply. "Boy, am I glad to see you. When I met you at work, I told John and Jim that you would be perfect for something we want to ask you." We all resumed the sitting positions we had enjoyed prior to Dan's arrival. Dan took a seat next to me on the campfire edge of the lean-to floor, while John simultaneously threw him a beer. --The 'cold one' I presume he had promised earlier.

"John, have you or Jim breached the subject of tonight's discussion with Andrew yet?" queried Dan.

"No," was their reply in unison.

"Well let's get right into it, O.K.?" responded Dan as he turned to look directly at me with an energetic and hopeful, yet earnest look of intensity. "Well, "he began as he 'popped' opened his beer can and met my eyes with his, "when you were at our office last month, you had complained to all of us about your family's excessive tax costs and the government's many unnecessary intrusions into your private life. You also complained about your family's inability to prosper due to an over-regulating, overbearing, and sometimes tyrannous government."

"Yea," I said cautiously.

"Well we feel the same way you do, and we have joined an organization that helps to ensure that our government maintains the Articles of the Constitution and our Bill or Rights, --those documents that delineate our rights of independence from any government, foreign or domestic. Our forefathers fought too damned hard and suffered too tremendously for us to let any of these rights erode away due to apathy in the wake of the over zealous and ambitious government we stand humbled before today. I enjoy the liberties that our ancestors have provided me through battle, and I hold the sacrifices they made in loss of life and pain endured as sacred to my way of life. The freedoms they earned for us from their past sufferings must never ever be eroded or discarded. To do so, would be a travesty to their memory."

"We are, Andrew, part of the U.S. Militia", interrupts John. And we want you to join our cause."

"NO WAY!" I retort, as I jump into a standing position. "I have enough problems."

This wouldn't be a 'problem' in your life --rather a blessing. You would finally be part of a group of U.S. citizens who believe in the same things that you do: --less government and the retention of the Constitution that safeguards our freedom as a people.

"Yea, --I agree with your basic premise of defending our liberties and preparedness against enemy attack, since I know from history that such an attack will occur again someday. But, the Militia has rebels at its fringes that disgrace your cause by perpetuating **illegal acts** against our government and its citizenry."

Those acts are not acts by the Militia," insists John. "Those acts are done by individuals who follow their own cause, not that of the Militia and then they are connected to us by the liberal media, thereby tarnishing our image unjustifiably. U.S. Militia members are to follow the laws of the land to enact change. We are a formidable voting force that stands behind the principles of the Constitution and the Bill of Rights. We would willingly die to protect our fellow countrymen from any invading military force. We are not a band of criminals, but rather a deep-rooted force that has been a part of the American scene since the 16th century. --Andrew, do you know that if you look up Militia in the dictionary it cites the United States National Guard as an example?"

Without my reply he continues, "The Militia is defined in the Dictionary as: 'A*ny army composed of citizens rather than professional soldiers, called out in the time of an emergency. It is divided into two classes, the organized militia, --now called the National Guard, and the reserve militia.'* We are that reserve militia that has been a part of America since the MinuteMen of the 16th century. We are ready to lobby and fight for our liberties against the threat of tyranny and oppression, whatever its origin."

John's deep voice booms with the crackle of the fire as Jim adds another log for burning. "Know who the first commanders were for a citizen militia in the United States? How do the names of George Washington, George Mason, and Samuel Adams ring to your ears?"

"Earnestly," I reply. "Tell me more."

As the campfire roared, John continued in a low, deep voice, which augmented the eeriness of this now cold, November evening. As he continued to talk, shadows from the campfire danced around the lean-to behind Dan's head, and crackling noises from the fire added a surreal and intense dimension to the conversation.

"In 1777, George Washington and George Mason organized the *Fairfax County Militia Association* in response to the British military occupation of Boston. Bostonians, who had earlier fled from Europe to obtain their freedom from a tyrannous government, now found themselves, once again, in the grips of an oppressive regime. British soldiers had confiscated all civilian weapons under the decree of British General Thomas Gage. The resulting militia battles at Lexington, Concord, and later at Bunker Hill, were the beginnings of the American Revolution for freedom".

"Other patriots such as Samuel Adams, of Boston, urged Americans everywhere to arm themselves and become instructed in military art. Adams even started his own militia group called *The Boston Chapter of the Sons of Liberty* as other militia associations sprung up throughout America."

John chimes in as one of our horses snorts in the background and Jim is seen stoking the fire using a small, green twig. "You've heard of the Minutemen of Massachusetts and several other 16th century New England Colonies haven't you?"

"Yea!" I respond.

"And you have heard of Ethan Allen and the Green Mountain Boys of Vermont, haven't you?" "Yes," I respond again.

"Well, they were all a part of the original American Militia that fought so effectively for the freedoms that we enjoy today."

"Like the freedom from slavery," Dan adds.

"--Or the freedom of speech," chimes in Jim.

"Or the right to vote, or no taxation without representation," I add, "but these are all words. In reality, no one is representing me in my needs to be free from the oppressive and excessive taxes that are limiting my prosperity and happiness. These have all become just hollow words taught to every U.S. citizen, but lacking true value. My individual tax rate of 59.1 percent does not allow me the opportunity of prosperity. It burdens me with nothing but despair and frustration."

"That is where we come in," cites Dan. "Join us, and we will help you lobby for your needs."

"I am too busy working every day to participate in any group. And besides, how do I help you lobby a government whose doors are only open from 9:00 A.M. to 5:00 P.M.? Those are my key working hours? I wouldn't have a job very long if I spent my daytime hours, Monday through Friday, lobbying government officials. Besides, I work until two in the morning as it is, --just to make ends meet."

"We know this," responds John, "that is why we are offering you our help. United as a large political force, our members can collectively fight for the maintenance of our basic freedoms."

"--Those rights that you feel you lack," adds Dan.

"I agree with your premise," I begin, with the fire light behind Dan's head fading as our campfire wanes. "But to fight the government you need the aid of politicians, not a militia force."

"That is true," responds Jim from atop his rock near the fire. "But what if our government becomes, by its continually increasing size, so large that it must become tyrannous and abusive to perpetrate itself further? Or what if we are invaded by a foreign government?"

Dead silence surrounds all until I interrupt the night's oppressive calm with the words, "I guess that's where the U.S. Military and the U.S. Militia come in."

"Let's turn in and let Andrew think about it," requests Jim from atop his rounded rock. "We have overwhelmed him with a torrent of information and I think it would be best for us to give him some time to digest what we've discussed."

Dan and John agree, and we simultaneously begin unrolling our bedrolls on the lean-to floor in preparation for the welcomed night of sleep awaiting us.

As the four of us lie side by side in the stillness of the night, my mind reflects on our discussion and my soul struggles in conflict. Although I have experienced financial oppression and anguish beset me by my government, I will not join their crusade in defense of my liberty for I am deprived the luxury of time by the very tyrant that I should rise to help cast down. I am too busy trying to make ends meet to spend time fighting an evasive and vast government bureaucracy. I lack both the funds and the time to make the slightest difference in the greater scheme of governmental affairs. Tears rise in my eyes as I think of my oppressed state in the private sector and the successes enjoyed by my comrades with government positions. "While I subscribe to the way of thinking of my three companions tonight, I will not join these friends of mine in their militia dealings," I thought. It is too complicated a task in my already over-complicated life, and it is too dangerous, since those in the militia have too tarnished an image.

As the cool and silent November night embraces me, I return my stare to the clear stars pulsating above me while simultaneously reflecting back to my joyous college days. In those glorious days I was so filled with self-righteousness, hope, desire, and dreams. I was a staunch 'capitalist' then. While studying for my business degree at the State of New

York Business College, in Proctor, my visions of wealth came from my view of a 'capitalistic' society in which no rules, regulations, or significant tax burdens existed to impede my successes in the business world. My successes in life would be derived from hard work and I would rise, unimpeded by any 'socialistic' type government or bureaucracy. My dreams were dashed upon receiving my first paycheck and realizing my government was much more intrusive than I had ever been lead to believe by parent, teacher, or peer.

When do we cease existing as a 'capitalistic' society and become a 'socialistic' society, I thought. Who decides and writes about the change in textbooks and newspapers throughout the world? Does the definition change with time? Is the definition of a 'capitalistic' society a relative term as compared to societies in the rest of the world, or does it possess a set meaning? If I was to define capitalism, I would suggest that a country thats populous pays less than 50% of its earnings in taxes is capitalistic. These people are left the majority of their hard earned money to spend on themselves."

My definition of a 'socialistic' society, would simply be one in which the citizenry pays more than fifty percent of its earnings to socialistic programs (the government). With this definition, our textbooks around the globe should be changed to note that America is now a socialistic versus a capitalistic society.

Are the principles of individual freedom and the rights of the individual destined for extinction as our country becomes more populated? I continued to reflect. As neighbors rise up around us, must we lose our individualism to appease the greater needs of the society in which we live? Isn't this called socialism? These concepts that have plagued me since the receipt of my first meager paycheck have risen up to become the demons which have destroyed all that I hold dear. I was taught the values of independence, liberty, and freedom in grade school only to find that these teachings were distorted myths. I have been betrayed by all.

"Are all brainwashed, ignorant, or just intentionally deceptive?", I ask myself.

When the collective forces of our government wrench a disproportionate percentage of our earnings from our family's hands, we have turned the corner from a 'capitalistic' to a 'socialistic' state.

"All in vain," I thought.

I have fought my war devoid of direction. Working hard and long hours will not overcome this tyrant that reaps my earnings, --it will only serve to provide him more. I would have been better off simply obtaining a government job out of college than trying to beat this Goliath that holds me to this miserable existence I now abhor.

I relish my independence, my freedom, and my liberties, but firmly believe that these three friends that accompany me here tonight have already lost their battles to a destiny that has already sealed their fate. We are no longer a 'capitalistic' society. We turned the corner to a 'socialistic' state years ago, and the ignorance of the masses and the propaganda of a system beset on self-protection join forces to seal our fate as a miserable and ignorant lot. We shall never again enjoy the freedoms we once possessed, nor shall we return to a majority in the private sector as our government continues to relish its position as the largest employer in the United States.

(See the following tables):

Government Agency	Percent of U.S. Employment
Local Government: City, Town, Village, & County Dog Warden, Tax Collector, Small Game Hunting License, Large Game Hunting License, Trapping License, Fishing License, Pistol Permit, Dog License. Building Permits & Zoning, Abstract & Title Bureau, Liquor License, Small Business Lic., Retail Sales Tax Certificate Bureau, City Sales Tax Collection Dept., City Council, Director of Finance, Director of Law, Engineer, Fire Dept. Health Dept. Industrial Waste & Cross Connection Control, Mayor, Municipal Court Probation, Probation Dept., Traffic & Criminal Div., Community Corrections Program, Civic and Small Claims, Div., Municipal Clerk of Courts, Municipal Court Judge, Park & Rec. Dept., Personnel Dir., Police Dept., Police Calls, Sanitation Dept.-refuge/ Garbage, Sewer Dept., Sanitation Garage, Street Dept. & Garage, Water Dept. Business Office, Water Treatment Plant, Water Works Shop, Garage, Cemetery, City Bldg., Fire & Emerg. Squad Training, Fire Dept. Business Office, Fire Chief, Town Hall, Trustees Office & Garage, Water Works Pumping Station, Building Inspector, Health Dept. Inspec., Fire Inspector, Electric Light & Water Billing, Electric Line Dept., Finance Dept., Industrial Development, Meter Department, Parks, Utility Billing Dept., Village Offices, Parks Maint., Village Administration, Birth & Death Certificates, Environmental Health Dept., Health Clinic, Health Ed., Plumbing Inspectors, Public Health Nursing, WIC Nutrition Program, Human Resources, Law Director, Litter Prevention & Recycling, Maintenance, Maintenance Fax, Neighborhood Youth Corps., Jails, Reservations, Crime Lab, Community Policing, Crime Prevention, Police Information, Juvenile Unit, Patrol Section, 911 Calls, Records, 911	

Calls, Records, Traffic Unit, Public Works Dir., Repair Garage, TDD/Hearing Impaired, Sanitation-Pickup, Treasurer, Ambulance Service, Public Trans. (Bus, Train, Subway), Light & Water Dept., Board of Trustees, Auditors, Road Dept. Garage, Coroner, County Board of Elections, County Commissioners, County Engineer, County Home for the Elderly, County Recorder, Dept. of Human Services, Social & Children Services, Day Care, Child Support Enforce., JOBS Dept., Landfill, Prosecuting Attorney, Prosecutor's Office, Regional Panning, Soil & Water Cons., Housing Authority, Agriculture Center, Land & Building Assessment, Personal Property Assessment, Real Estate Assessment, Weights & Measures, Building Codes & Regulations, Drug/Alcohol Program, Forensic Center, Central Purch., Abuse Complaints, Adoptions, Foster Care, Volunteer Programs, Child Protection, Court of Appeals, Divorce Court, Divorce Filing, Dog Pound, Drug Hotline, Domestic Violence Shelter, Early Intervention, Emergency Mgt. Agency, Welfare Fraud Hotline, Children's Health Insurance, Adult Protective Svc., Humane Society, Private Industry Council, Law Library, Local Emergency Planning, Maintenance, Mental Health Board, Microfilm Center, County Info. Phone Line, County Newhope Center, County Preschool, Risk Mgt., Sheriff, Dept. Bureau, Food Pantry, Homeless Shelter, Maintenance & Grounds, City Schools, Tax Map Dept., Local Portion of the Public Libraries, County Zoo, Art Museum, Museum, County Hospitals, Nursing Homes, Local Retired Govnt. Employees on Pension & Retirement Program Benefits & Insurance…………………………………………………	6.1%
Total Local U.S. Government Paycheck Recipients (% of U.S. Work Force):	**6.1%**

State Government:	
Boat Licensing, Snowmobile Licensing, Pistol Permits, State Alcohol Licensing Bureau, Motor Vehicle Dept., Deputy Registrar of Motor Vehicles, Motor Vehicle Licenses, Driver Exam Station, Marriage Licenses, Notary License, Small Business Sales Tax Collection License, Lottery Licensing Bureau, Lottery, Lottery Treasurer, Lottery Administration, Lottery Advertising Task Force Department, Bureau of Vocational Rehabilitation, Highway Patrol, Pistol Permit, Department of Development, Employment Services, Highway Patrol, Industrial Commission, Park Commission, Correctional Facilities, Prisons, Adult Parole Authority, Department of Taxation, Treasurer, Department of Transportation, Rehabilitation Services, Veterans Employment Services, Workers Compensation Bureau, Highway Maint., Highway Construction, Bridge Maintenance & Construction, Tunnel Maintenance and Construction, Snow Removal, Public Utilities Commission, Consumer Inquiries, Attorney General, Public Utilities Commission, Maintenance & Grounds, Staff State Judicial System, State Administrators & Politicians, Legislature, Governor, State Services (where the state div. for the handicapped and prisons allow their wards to make products, which the state then buys back. I.e. Furniture, cleaning supplies, soap, license plates). This division competes with the private sector. Harness Racing Commission, Gaming/Casino (Gambling) Commission, Weights & Measures, Bar Association, State Portion of the Public Libraries, Purchasing, Court of Appeals, Auto Title, State Examiner, Coroner, Agriculture, Soil & Water Consv., Farm Home Low Income Loans, Aid to Dependent Children, Small Business Loans, Minority Business Loan Dept., College Loans & Administration, Supplies Warehouse & Trans., Road and Bridge Tolls & Administration, Census Bureau, State Medical Hospitals, State Psych. Hospitals nurses-staff-maintenance & grounds, Plus all State Workers Receiving a Pension or Disability Check......................	4.5%

National Guard Bases, National Guard Accounting and Finance, Aircraft Maintenance, Equip. Maint., Supplies, Civil Engineering, Flight Operations, ID Cards/Personnel, Logistics Mgt., Medical Squadron, Security Police, Maintenance & Grounds……………………………	0.1%
Unemployment Compensation Bureau Recipients, Staff, & Administrators……………..…….	7.0%
Public Schools, Colleges & Universities, Teachers/Professors, Substitute Teachers/Asst. Professors, Cafeteria Services, Maintenance, Building & Grounds, Coaching Staff, Admin., School Board Supplies and Building Space, Staff, Textbooks & Maintenance, Scholastic Testing Services (i.e. SAT's), School Nurse, Teachers Paid for Continuing Ed…...…..………..	1.0%
State Employees on Retirement Pension and Insurance Programs……………………...…………	1.6%
State Welfare Paycheck Recipients……………………………………...…………………………	3.0%
Total State U.S. Government Paycheck Recipients (% of U.S. Work Force):	**17.2%**

Federal Government: Washington Politicians, Congress, Legislature, President, Vice President, Secretary of State, Foreign Ambassadors, Foreign Embassies, The Judicial Branch, Supreme Court, Staff & Clerks, Building Maintenance & Grounds, The Federal Trade Commission, Federal Deposit Insurance Corp., Federal Emergency Management, Federal Extension Services, Federal Home Loan Bank Board, Federal Housing Authority, Federal Maritime Commission, Federal Mediation and Conciliating Service, Copy Right Office, Power Commission, Federal Reserve System, Federal Savings & Loan Association, National Dept. Loan & Pay off Department, Federal Trade Commission, Occupational Safety & Health Administration (OSHA), Federal Wage & Hour Administration, Law Dept., Ethics Office, Printing Offices, Convention Services, Security, Parks Administration, Federal Parks Maintenance & Mgt., Environmental Protection Agency (EPA), Re-election Campaign Fund Raising Committee, The Senate, The House, Polls & Voting Oversight Agencies, Presidential Security, Federal Building Security, Presidential Plane Maintenance, President Logistics & Reservation Staff, The Federal Bureau of Investigation (FBI), Secret Service (Throughout the World), Federal Drug Task Force, Drug Policing Agency, U.S. Boarder Patrol, Immigration Services., Internal Revenue Service, Federal Tax Forms Agency, Federal Tax Information Services, TTD/Hearing Impaired, Farm Services Agency, Housing and Urban Development Admin. (HUD), Natural Res. Conservation Service, Vehicles Maint., Score-Service Corp. of Retired Executives, Federal Aviation Administration, Airport Traffic Control, Bureau of Alcohol, Tobacco, and Firearms, U.S. Customs, U.S. Attorney General, Department of Agriculture,	

- Continued -	
Agriculture Inspection/Marketing-Commodities and Food, Food Inspectors (USDA), Biological Research, Centers of Disease Control and Prevention, Dept. of Commerce, Dept. of the Interior, House of Representatives, Antitrust, Consumer Hotlines, Aviation Safety Commission, Consumer Product Safety Commission, Consumer Protection Agency, Federal Trade Commission (FTC). Housing Counsel for Home Buyers, Cultural Resources, Dams & Dam Safety, Deaf-Hard of Hearing-and Speech Disabled Assistance, Health and Human Services Division of Discrimination Complaints, Education Dept., Fish & Wildlife Service, National Flood Insurance Program, Health Care Information Services, Hearings and Appeals Bureau, Hepatitis Information, Wild Horse & Burro Adoption Program, Immigra-tion Court, Immunization, American Indian Programs and Services, Labor Relations, Law Enforcement, Federal Union Negotiators, Counterfeit Merchandise Law Enforcement, Lead Poisoning Bureau, Federal Employees Group Life Insurance Program, Education Loans, Housing Loans, Maps, Marshal Svc. Maternal & Child Health Info., Medicare, Mental Health Information, Prisons, Mental Institutions, Shelters, Mineral Resources, The U.S. Mint, National Aeronautic and Space Administration, Nuclear Regulatory Commission, Passports, Peace Corps, Personnel Management Office, Primary Care Information, Migrant Health, Bureau of Public Debt, Railroad Retirement Board, Railroad Supplemental Funding Administration, Recreation Department, Presidential Commission of Health, Runaway National Switchboard, Rural Development Cooperative Services, Lock and Bridge Mgt., Highway Management., Federal Highway Administration, U.S. Savings Bonds, Small Business Administration, Smoking and Health Information, Social Security Administration, Retail Liquor Deal Tax & Regulation Department, Telemarketing on Consumer Protection Issues, Transportation Disaster Response, Traveler's International Health Advisory, Visitor Centers, Warranties, Water Resources, Public Broadcasting Commission, Wildlife Fish & Game Commission, Women's Health Information, Central Intelligence Agency (CIA), Food & Drug Administration (FDA), U.S. Census Bureau, Commerce Department, Department of Labor, Federal Prisons, Plus all Retired Federal Employees Collecting Pension Benefits and Insurance..	19.1%

U.S. Military (All Branches) Including Recruiting Offices, All U.S. & Foreign Bases, National Guard-Federal Operations, Defense Department, Defense Logistics, Quality Assurance, Buildings & Grounds Maintenance, Equipment Maintenance, Equipment & Supplies Storage, Military Equipment & Supplies Purchasing Offices, Staff, Administration, Enlisted and Support Personnel, The Selective Service System, Filming and Educational Department, Training Personnel, Department of Veterans Affairs, Veterans Benefits to Dependents of Disabled Veterans, Military Pension Programs for Both Regular Military and National Guard Personnel, The Coast Guard, Also Military Disability Check Recipients, Coast Guard Pension Benefit Recipients……………………………………………………	8.1%
U.S. Postal Services, Post Offices, Warehouse Management, Transportation & Delivery, Sorting Services, Postal Inspector, Post Masters, Postal Carriers, Buildings and Grounds Personnel, Building Maintenance, Equipment Maintenance, Delivery Truck & Plane Maintenance, Training Staff, Clerks, Staff, Accounting, and Retired Postal Workers on Retirement pensions. Also Disabled Postal Workers Collecting a Federal Check……………...	1.5%
Total Federal U.S. Paycheck Recipients (% of total U.S. work force):	**28.7%**

Total U.S. Government Employees Paycheck Recipients For the Year Ending 2004…….	**52%**

As I reflect on the government employment statistics, which are burnt into my head, I let out a sigh and mumble, "fifty-two freakin' percent". How many more U.S. employees will the government gain before it admits that we have become a socialistic state? Further, we must ask ourselves if we are slowly becoming a communist regime, where workers predominately work for the government. With a collective individual tax rate of 59.1 percent, and with the U.S. Government's employment figures now reaching a whopping fifty-two percent, there is no way that one can argue that capitalism is the driving force of our economy. That argument was factually and statistically defeated over a decade ago. But, the government, that wants to protect itself from exposure, will never admit that we have become a socialistic society. Why should a rat expose itself, when it can feed heartily and undisturbed in the shadows.

I chuckle to myself in disgust as I reflect back again to my college years. I remember reading Marx's Communist Manifesto. In that key document of the socialist/communist movement, Karl Marx and his comrade by the name of Friedrich Engles, suggested that the key to the socialist/ communist movement was the employee's union[6]. Through their voting power (collective *"political supremacy"*[7]), he argued that a united worker could overthrow the capitalistic class society in an attempt to make all workers equal.[8] It could be done, he said *"by degrees"*[9] and he predicted that all capitalistic societies would eventually turn to socialism/ communism. *"Now and then,"* he said, *"the workers are victorious, but only for a time. The real fruit of their battles lies, not in the immediate result, but in the ever-expanding*

---

[6] Bender, Frederich L., <u>*Karl Marx THE COMMUNIST MANIFESTO*</u>, W.W. Norton Company, N.Y., 1988, p.63, 74, 86.

[7] Ibid, p. 74.

[8] Ibid, pp. 63, 74, 86.

[9] Ibid, p. 74.

union of the workers." I'll never forget the final words of his manifesto, *"WORKING MEN OF ALL COUNTRIES, UNITE!"* The Federal Teachers Union, Federal Employee's Union, and the other various local government employee unions have become that united force. And through their voting power they have inevitably grown from forty percent of our U.S. work force to fifty-two percent over the past fifty year period. We will never again have the voting power to reduce their size significantly. Let us just hope that they don't grow even larger, or revolt by the capitalist and private citizens will be the only method to oust them from their collectively oppressive mass.

Those in the government, whom I know, gloat when they take my hard-earned tax money and they can't understand why I don't want to pay them even more in taxes, by voting for their many causes. While at the same time, they are unwilling to admit that we have become a socialistic society, as opposed to one based on the capitalistic principals of small government and expanded individual freedoms. This governmental mass knows that it is still too soon to change our textbooks to reveal its new nature. They are embarrassed and apprehensive, I'm sure, to reveal their true essence, for to do so would cause rebellion and disgust by the private sector. Our government has risen to become a masked monster, but I, for one, can see through the disguise. Rather than expose themselves, they will take Marx's advice. He had advocated in his Communist Manifesto, that the united union workers should *"wrest, by degrees, all capital from the bourgeoisie* (the private sector), *to centralize all instruments of production in the hands of the State"*[10]. They've accomplished their goal with much stealth, I thought, as I gazed into the stars before falling to sleep.

---

[10] Bender, Frederich L., *Karl Marx THE COMMUNIST MANIFESTO*, W.W. Norton & Company, N.Y., 1988, p.74.

The hour of 6:00 A.M. came much too soon as we reluctantly greeted the morning with an egg and venison breakfast cooked over an all-too-smoky fire. The hour of 7:00 A.M. saw three of us on horseback in search for the elusive game that we had come to hunt, while Dan scurried through the dew soaked woods to his Jeep, parked two kilometers away on an old logging road. By day's end, John had shot his second deer. It was a six-point buck this time. Jim got his deer, a four-point buck. And I departed devoid of venison, but rich with camaraderie and engaging conversation.

"Thank you guys, for a very enjoyable three day adventure. I will think about our conversation," were my departing words, after stabling my horse, at the Cindrich family barn. I then walked toward my auto/van in preparation for my return to my Ohio office/residence in Decorah.

Upon arriving at my Decorah office and checking my fax machine for orders, two of the several orders received were from *Cindrich and Company*. Both purchase orders were signed, Jim Fletcher. These gifts from the Cindrich's, and Jim, were icing on the cake from an enjoyable and intellectually stimulating three day hunt in Western Ohio. It is now back to work for me. I have orders to write and bills to pay.

(Source: A sketch by Andrew Henry, from his personal diary dated 1998-2004).

"A well-regulated militia, being necessary to the security of a free State, the right of the people to keep and bear arms, shall not be infringed."

Second Amendment to the Constitution of the United States *(1791)*.

This quotation and notation was entered into Andrew's diary on February 20, 2004 at 7 A.M. He entered this quotation from memory, at the age of 49.

Chapter Eight: The Invasion

Three months after my hunting expedition with the Cindrichs, I found myself daydreaming about our excursion while driving east down Ohio's Route 30. I was on my way to Pittsburgh to make sales calls, but since my first sales meeting in that city was not scheduled until 9:00 A.M., and it was now only 7:00 A.M., I had plenty of time to think. As I drove up each hill, the engine of my autovan labored and lost momentum, but the explanation was a simple one. I had not only loaded my van with ample product samples for a week long sales trip, but had added personal belongings to the load, since I planned to arrive at my upstate New York residence by week's end. A car with 149,000 miles cannot be expected to surge up the hills of eastern Ohio fully loaded without a struggle. After pondering about the Cindrich's militia proposal for a time, my thoughts unintentionally shifted to a completely dissimilar topic, as I drove. The issue of 'power and influence' took control of my bearing as my thoughts meandered toward a deliberation on that issue. It seems that my customers who command the greatest power, I thought, will do anything to maintain it. Those who want power, will do practically anything to obtain it.

And the rest of us fall victim to these masters of power and influence, in many ways, throughout our life.

Most of the highly powerful men I've known in business, have been the most deceptive and dishonest people I have ever met. I have always experienced the most ethical transgressions while dealing with my largest and wealthiest distributors. The owners of these distributorships would exaggerate the prices they paid from my competitors in their attempt to obtain more aggressive pricing from me. They would even lie about damaged merchandise in their warehouse to obtain an unjustified credit on their account, in their effort to earn unjust profits. I had a few large distributors who even lied about their bid contract sales, in an effort to reap unearned credits against their accounts. They would request a bid for a bogus governmental agency, and submit monthly credit requests for these contrived contracts. When I caught these business owners in their dishonest deeds, they would predictably claim ignorance. Or another trick, well mastered through years of use, would cast them in an act of self-righteous, indignant, denial. "How dare you question me," would be their response when caught in a moral transgression. Or "Who do you think you are?" would be another attempt of reversing the blame to anyone who would be intimidated enough to accept it. These masters of deception were very convincing, since they had spent years developing their craft. Fortunately, as soon as they would realize that their games had minimal effect on me, their attempts at manipulation and extortion would diminish to a tolerable level. I would stand my ground on principle, even at the sacrifice of some business. Unfortunately, this tack, based on moral convictions, bares a lofty cost. For each time you refuse to acquiesce, you lose future opportunities to competitors who will willingly cave to the demands of the unscrupulous.

Now why, I continued thinking, do these men of power and wealth need to cheat? It is not the money they need, since they are already worth millions. Perhaps it is because they cheat and lie that they have the money and power. For I have always thought that atheists can achieve anything they desire, since they are held accountable to no superior being. Whatever they can get away with is appropriate. But if they are atheistic in nature, why do these swindlers attend church? Is it simply part of an act that provides them further glory and power in their temporal lives? I am not much of a churchgoer myself, since I obtain more meaning simply reading the Bible in private, but when I do attend I am appalled at the many powerful hypocrites surrounding me. I, too, am a hypocrite to my religion, since I live a life far from the staunch commands of the Bible, but I am not an atheist. But many of the men of wealth and power seen in the church, I know are atheists in disguise. Prior to entering the sacred doors of their place of worship, they were liars, adulterers, and cheats. Then, after the sermon, they return to the streets of their cities, unchanged. While in church, I imagine them hypocritically viewing the cross of Christ with their left eye, while scanning the room with their right in search for opportunity or acknowledgement of their presence. They are not there for the love of God, I conclude, but to be seen by man. Most have never once read the Bible cover to cover, both the New Testament and the Old Testament combined *(or the Koran, etc)*. And unfortunately, to the determent of the truly pious parishioners, they receive the attention of the church that declares them 'pillars of the community' as a result of their generous donations designed for such an effect. *"And again I say unto you, it is easier for a camel to go through the eye of a needle, than for a rich man to enter into the kingdom of God*[11]*,"* are the biblical

[11] King James Version, <u>The Ryrie Study Bible</u>, Moody Press, Chicago, IL, 1976, p. 1373, *(Matthew, 19:24)*.

words that ring true to my ears whenever cast down from the pulpit. It is not that I am envious of those with money, it is that I despise their hypocrisy in church, since I have witnessed their true demonic essence in the world outside.

In contrast to my wealthiest and most influential distributors, my most honest distributors are typically my smallest accounts. Their honesty supersedes their need to earn a profit. Even if it costs them money, they would tell me of an error I had made when billing them. These honest men, I thought, would always have a difficult time becoming larger or more influential than they already are in their respective markets. Their moral fabric will disallow them from achieving the competitive size their unethical counterparts have obtained.

Is the relationship between power and lack of ethics in business similar to its relationship in our governmental sector? If so, I thought, than we are probably ruled by many of the greatest deceivers on earth, since it appears that the most unscrupulous rise to the most powerful positions. Adolf Hitler, Benito Mussolini, Attila the Hun, General Hannible Barca, Joseph Stalin, Saddam Hussein, and Slobodan Milosevic are a few of the many names that come to mind when asserting that statement.

I'll never forget the multi-millionaire's son, who once revealed to me a hideous truth my first summer after high school graduation. He had graduated from an out-of-state private school for the elite, and I, from a local public school. We were both lifeguards that summer and, during one of our after-hour lifeguard parties, he had finished a heated debate that we had been engaged in with a comment that has lived with me these thirty-one years hence.

"You will never rise to a level above your current 'middle-class status'," he had told me, "because you are too ethical." He continued, "The poor will stay poor since they value sex and liquor more than education and because their social and family networks encourage blue-collar work as opposed to education. Those in the middle-class, like you," he said, "are limited in your abilities by your middle class ethics beset on you by a God you do not even know. The rich of this world are takers. --We are not limited by the ethical standards of the middle class."

In watching that man prosper for the past thirty-one years I've learned all to well that his convictions were true. Working for him led to the ruin of many good people and wonderful families. And those who dealt with him, soon learned that they would be the recipients of the short-end of the stick. He was known as a liar who would do anything for power or money, yet he prospered even with this self-admitted transgressions against man and God.

"Oops, gotta' get gas," I blurted as noticed I was devoid of fuel while casually gazing at the speedometer.

I was somewhere between my Decorah office/ apartment and Pittsburgh, when I veered off Interstate 30 onto the car mat of a truck-stop service station. As I began fueling my autovan, I noticed that people around me were acting strangely. I could not discern the origin of their odd behavior no matter how much I rotated my head to view the scene around me. There was no sign of smoke or fire in the area, and they were not acting panicked enough for their distress to be driven by that possibility. I searched the sky for signs of the approach of bad weather or hurricane. --No gray sky or threatening weather could be observed. In contrast, the morning sky gave all the signs of the approach of a perfect weather day. There were sporadic white buffed clouds sparsely dotting the light blue background of our beautiful morning sky, but no ominous phenomenon could be detected. Why were these people acting so strange?

It was as if all around me were mentally preoccupied or confused. They did not run in panic, nor did they seem cognitive of the source of their odd behavior. They seemed to be completely distraught, but the source of their anguish could not be readily identified.

I hurriedly returned the nozzle of my fuel hose to the pump and walked to the service station. Upon entering I saw a crowd of approximately fifteen people watching a television monitor suspended from the ceiling in the trucker's dining area. Their eyes were glued to a news report.

"Oh, great," I thought, "we're back at war with some foreign country."

As I walked toward the group, a thin man wearing a gray beard and truck driving garb passed me, shaking his head and sputtering; "we're freakin' in it now."

As I met the group before the monitor, I stood with them and continued viewing the grim scene on the screen. Not only was it a war, but it was a war on our shores.

"To repeat the information from our 7:00 o'clock newscast," the news anchorman announced, "the United States has been invaded. H-bombs have been dropped on the cities of New York, Washington, Los Angeles, and San Francisco. Nuclear missiles, launched from offshore nuclear submarines, have hit Air Force Bases on all three U.S. coasts. Fighter plane losses and severe casualties in Air Force personnel have been reported at the following Air Force Bases:

Mc Guire Air Force Base, Fort Dix, New Jersey
Bolling Air Force Base, Washington, D.C.
Andrews-Mead Air Force Base, Meadows, Maryland
Langley Air Force Base, Poquoson, Virginia.
Dover Air Force Base, Dover, Delaware
Barksdale Air Force Base, Boissier City, Louisiana

Mather Air Force Base, Sacramento, California
Castle Air Force Base, Winton, California
Vandenberg Air Force Base, Surf, California
Edwards Air Force Base, Edwards, California
The Naval Air Station in Lamoore, California
Beale Air Force Base, Linda, California.
Travis Air Force Base, Fairfield, California
Los Angeles Air Force Base, Los Angeles, California
Goodfellow Air Force Base, San Angelo, Texas
Randolf Air Force Base, San Antonio, Texas
Kelly Air Force Base, San Antonio, Texas
The U.S. Naval Air Station at Corpus Christi, Texas
Dyess Air Force Base, Abilene, Texas
Berstrom Air Force Base, Cedar Creek, Texas
Laughlin Air Force Base, Del Rio, Texas
Sheppard Air Force Base, Wichita Falls, Texas
Web Air Force Base, Big Spring, Texas
Biggs Army Airfield, Elpaso, Texas
Brook, Air Force Base, San Antonio, Texas
Dallas Naval Air Station, Dallas, Texas
Carswell Air Force Base, Dallas, Texas
Tyndall Air Force Base, CedarGrove, Florida
Eglin Air Force Base, Fort Walton Beach, Florida
Patric, Air Force Base, Cape Canaveral, Florida.
MacDill Air Force Base, Tampa, Florida
Homestead Air Force Base, Princeton, Florida

We know that U.S. Navy submarines are in full engagement with the vessels of the attacking forces. As enemy aircraft carriers and battle ships approach our shores, from far off in the ocean, they are being met with equal force by our military. Information throughout the country has been sporadic, scrambled, and confused. We will keep you abreast of further developments as best we can. For now, seek shelter in the nearest fall out shelter." The scene on the television monitor now changes from the newscaster at CQB national television headquarters to a local station.

"For a list of shelters in your area," the commentator commands, "turn your radio to the local Emergency Alert System station for news and instructions."

The television scene on the monitor returns to the CQB headquarters, where the news anchor continues the broadcast.

"Repeat; The United States has been invaded. Information is limited. Seek shelter immediately."

H o l y C O W, I thought, I knew this day would come. --It was just a matter of time. Two more people left the crowd and briskly walked for the exit door. I threw a twenty-dollar bill on the cashier's counter, since she was busy preparing the store for closing, and then exited to my car. When I drove onto Interstate 30, the traffic volume had already increased. While continuing east toward Pittsburgh, I immediately began thinking of the best drive route back to my upstate New York residence. I had to get home to help my wife and daughter.

Oh boy, I thought. I have to help my elderly in-laws as well.

"H o l y Cow," I sputtered. "I new this would happen someday. --I daw-gawnit' knew this would happen someday".

As I sputtered insanities in every direction, from inside my vehicle, I frustratingly thought of how to get home quickly. There was just no way of getting there fast enough by car.

It's an eight-hour drive no matter which route I take, I thought.

In my desperation to find a quicker way home to my family, I thought of John Cindrich and his militia group. Perhaps someone in his organization would be willing to fly me to my residence despite the immanent risks of radiation exposure from the New York City nuclear bombardment. John's paper warehouse was only an hour an ten minutes ahead of me. I could continue driving east on Route 30 and then drop down to John's paper warehouse via Route 45. I could be there by about 8:30 A.M.

As my odometer speed climbed, I began passing people on this four lane highway. I did not worry about the traffic police stopping me, since I knew they would be preoccupied with more important tasks. Then, I spontaneously slammed on my brakes to turn into a service station where I quickly saw a pay phone in the service yard. I called The Cindrich Company.

"Is John there?" I asked. "This is an emergency."

I knew that John's receptionist, Karen, would not put me through to John if I told her I was Andrew from NPM. John answered the phone with, "Colonel Cindrich, what's up?" "John, it's me," I replied. "Sorry to interrupt, but I'm hoping that your militia group can get me to my wife and daughter in upstate New York. I'm on Route 30, just east of Dalton right now, and will be at your place in an hour. Could any of your guys fly me to my home? --You're my only hope! My car radio says that all of the public airports are shut down."

"Andrew, I will help you, but you have got to calm down and talk efficiently. We don't have much time," John states. "Tell me their physical address."

"3360 Main Street, Logan, NY," I replied.

"Phone number?"

"607 332-5529," I blurted.

"Phones may not work, but I am sure that we have some people with shortwave radios in that area. We'll contact them from here, and have them get over to your house to take your wife and daughter to a bomb shelter. They will be taken to a militia-built bomb shelter, which is much safer than a public shelter. In addition, they will have armed militia men to protect them and explain things to them."

"Thanks John," I responded. "I will keep driving and hopefully be home in six hours. How will I find out where your men have taken them?"

"There's no time for that," John replied. "The radioactive fallout from both the New York City bombings and New Jersey Air Force base bombings could reach the area of your residence well before your arrival. You would be driving yourself right into a silent killer," John stated.

"I need to get home." was my reply.

"Andrew, you said that you're driving this way anyway, correct?"

"Yes," I responded with a questioning tone.

"Just drive past the paper company, since we will have evacuated this place by then. We'll be up at my parents' farm, where you and I went hunting a few months ago. Meet me up there, and we will put you up in our bomb shelter. You can talk to your wife and child from there, via our short wave radio, if the phones don't work. Drive up the farmstead road to my parents' farmhouse and old barn. Park behind my parents' house, and walk into the barn. We'll be in the barn making preparations.

"Thanks a lot John, that makes sense," I replied. "I'll see you up there in an hour."

After hanging up the receiver, I immediately attempted calling home, but the line was dead, just as John had suggested it might be.

My head became dizzy and flushed as I sat in my idling car at the drive-up pay phone. What could be happening to my wife and daughter at this very moment, I thought to myself, in a confused and zombie-like state. I also wished that I still had my portable car-phone, but I stopped using that expensive luxury after my bankruptcy five years ago.

A cell phone may not work anyway, I mentally consoled myself. I have heard that nuclear blasts send out an electromagnetic pulse that can severely damage ground-based cell phone network systems. Who knows, all I know right now is that I've got to get to the Cindrich farm and then home to my wife and daughter in upstate New York, I thought. As I began driving away from the pay phone, there was an immediate, loud, and aggressive horn beeping just in front of me. As I swerved to avoid another motorist, I realized that it was another driver forcing his way to the phone that I had just left. His agitated state served to further unravel my nerves and emotions. I re-entered highway 30 enroute to the Cindrich farm and sped down the four-lane highway at 80 miles per hour trying to reduce the hour and a half drive to the Cindrich's to an hour.

The next hour was the longest hour of my life. I had frustratingly tried to contact home by stopping at any unoccupied pay phone I passed along the way. --The lines to upstate New York remained dead, on all my attempts. The guilt that riddled my being during this exhausting drive to the Cindrichs was overwhelming.

If I could just be there with my wife and daughter to help them out, I thought.

"I need to be there. Darn it! I N E E D TO BE THERE! ! !" I yelled from inside the car as I sped down the highway.

It was 8:45 A.M. when I drove into the Cindrich farmstead. Other confused and hectic drivers, combined with my stopping at various pay phones on the way, had delayed my arrival. I pulled behind the large farmhouse as John had instructed, and then ran to the barn, carrying only my briefcase, which contained my personal phone book and my attaché case containing toiletry items. Upon entering the barn, I asked John if he had been able to help my wife.

"Everything is set," John said. "Don't worry, we've taken care of everything."

John continued to explain that he had reached a militia cell positioned three kilometers outside the rural hamlet of Clawson, New York. He did so via the shortwave radio at his office. Since the militia group was located only fifteen minutes from my wife's home, they told John that they would send two of their men to her residence to get both my wife and daughter. "If they find your wife and daughter, they will take them to their Clawson area based bomb shelter," he said. "They added that; 'no more civilians would be allowed', so I sincerely hope that there is no one else at your house besides your wife and daughter."

"No," I responded. "My in-laws are on Peck Lake, but by now I am sure that they've found their own shelter at a public facility. But how can I find out if your men have found my wife and daughter?" I quickly asked John.

"Come on, we can call them right now."

John hurriedly walked across the barn floor. We passed Jim Fletcher and Dan Cindrich along the way. They were making some sort of preparations near an old tractor. Off to one side were two children and two women. I presumed that they were John's wife and two children accompanied by Dan's wife, since Jim Fletcher was single. At the barn's center, we walked down some wooden stairs to a concrete pad. There were unoccupied cow stanchions on each side, and from that point we continued walking to the end of that basement area. At the end, we took an abrupt left and opened a large, rotted, wooden door. Debris fell as the door opened and cobwebs abounded along the entranceway. We walked down three steps onto a dirt floor. Ahead of me stood what appeared to be a thirteen-meter passageway with fieldstone sides and a concrete roof. Halfway down this musty corridor were old electric lights which dimly lit our way. As we continued down this tunnel, I noticed old electric wires and an old, one-inch standard measurement, cast iron pipe running lengthwise along the wall to my right. The pipe and wires were both at shoulder height.

As we reached the end of the tunnel I could see a large, steel door. John opened the door by lifting a latch and pushing in. The rusty door squeaked upon opening and we stepped one step down into his bomb shelter. The shelter was approximately 6.5 meters long x 4.7 meters wide. It had another large metal door positioned half way down on the right. On each side of the shelter were worn, wooden benches running lengthwise along the wall. The benches were probably worn from their use as part of a dairy parlor and shower room when the farm was in active use as a dairy farm. The old, black, calf-high farm boots standing in the corner along with an old pair of farmer's coveralls hanging on a wall hook, served to confirm my conclusions on the room's past use.

The bench along the right wall ran to the doorjamb in the center of the room, stopped, and then continued running from the far side of the doorjamb to a distance of approximately 1.5 meters from the far end of our bunker. The bench running along the left side of the shelter ran half way down the wall. It stopped at a metal shower stall. At the far end of the bunker was a refrigerator positioned in the left corner. To the right of the refrigerator was a small counter and then a four-burner stove. To the right of the stove was another small counter that ran to a double sink. To the right of the sink the counter top continued another meter to the wall containing a main circuit breaker and fuse box. Cabinets were positioned both above and below the sink.

John immediately walked over to a shortwave radio seated on the far end of the wooden bench, to our right, and began turning the knob. Using a sequence of Morse code dots and dashes, he began sending a message. Five minutes passed with no reply. John turned the dial slightly and tried again. Immediately the noise of a returned sequence of dots and dashes filled the bunker while John hurriedly scribbled out their meaning.

"They got 'em," John announced, as I immediately began to shake uncontrollably and had to sit down on the rough plank bench to my right. "The militia cell in Clawson, New York has your wife and daughter safely protected in their underground bomb shelter."

"Thank God," I announced with my head in my hands. "Thank God!"

(Source: A sketch by Andrew Henry, from his personal diary dated 1998-2004).

"From the east to the west blow the trumpet to arms. Through the land let the sound of it flee; Let the far and the near all unite, with a cheer, In defense of our Liberty Tree."

-Thomas Paine, The Liberty Tree
(July 1775).

Written in Andrew Henry's Diary on February 21, 2004, during his second morning at the bomb shelter site. This quotation was entered by Andrew sometime between 2:00 A.M. and 3:45 A.M.

Chapter Nine: The Enemy

Our group spent this first day above ground readying the fallout shelter, the equipment, and our guns. Since the Geiger counter in John's possession indicated that radiation levels had not increased, in our area, we were able to work 'topside'. Unfortunately, that was not the case for my wife and daughter in upstate New York. They were cramped into their fallout shelter with twelve other people. The fact that I could not talk to them directly, via John's shortwave radio, was becoming increasingly frustrating; but John had explained that the distance was too great for verbal communications. His response was that he had to communicate using Morse code to reach my wife's shelter, due to the long distance involved. I didn't really know what a transceiver was, but I took him at his word that verbal communication with my family, via shortwave, was out of the question. He did add however, that we may get lucky some night and reach them by voice, but he doubted that possibility with the amateur band equipment we were using. He promised that he would try again late this evening, when conditions would be more favorable for a direct line verbal communication or relayed verbal transmission.

The women, the children, and I spent the remainder of the day frantically stocking our fallout shelter with food and supply provisions as instructed by John. John, meanwhile, spent most of the day in the shelter communicating to other militia cell groups by shortwave radio.

At 3:00 P.M., John left his many notes on the card table that we had set up for him next to his radio set, to take a break topside for a while. As the rest of us continued our preparation efforts, I saw John check the air for radiation using an old 1964 era, Civil Defense, radar detector. John referred to it as a 'Victoreen Radiological Survey Meter'. While holding that meter toward the ground with his right hand, he simultaneously held a pen-type detector to the air with his left.

"What's that, John?" I asked as I stopped outside the open barn door to ascertain what he was doing.

"I'm checking for radiation."

"I thought that was what the 'Victoreen' box radiation detector did."

"It does Andrew, but I'm running a second check with this 'pen' detector. I call it a 'pen' detector because it is shaped like a large pen and it clips to your shirt pocket like a pen would. It is a contemporary device," he added, "manufactured by Bendix and used by nuclear power plant workers for the convenient and quick checking of air during their workday."

"If this red light at the end comes on," he added as he aimed the 'pen' detector towards me like a flashlight, "then we're in trouble." As I stared into the end of the detector I could see a small light bulb the size of a pen-flashlight bulb protruding out in my direction.

"See that bulb?" John asked.

"Yes."

"Take this detector and check it periodically when you are outside. If you see that light bulb light up, alert everyone so that we can run to the shelter, 'cause it means that we're all in big trouble".

"Okay," I said, as I apprehensively took the device from John.

"Don't worry," he said. "I've got more of them, and we will all be testing periodically. The task won't be your sole responsibility, but I'd appreciate your help."

"Yes sir!" I responded with a smile and salute and then turned and walked away giggling at my own sick attempt at humor during this time of crisis.

By 5:00 P.M. all seemed safe at our farmhouse haven in eastern Ohio, so Colonel Cindrich relieved us of our duties at '1700' and allowed us to wash up for dinner.

John had stated that it was '1700' but my watch showed 5:00 P.M.

As we joined Mrs. Cindrich and the kids at the dining room table, we observed a wonderful-looking farm meal (on the table) accompanied by the appetizing aroma of freshly mashed potatoes, buttered peas, and pot roast. I was ravenous after a day of frantic work devoid of meals or snacks, and the warm aroma of the meal was welcomed.

"The meal looks and smells great, Mrs. Long," John's wife remarked to Mrs. Cindrich's live-in caretaker who had prepared our feast.

"Thank you," replied Mrs. Long. "Now everyone, please sit down and eat before it gets cold."

As the last of the group was seated, John could be seen at the end of the table directly opposite his elderly mother. With bowed head and clasped hands, John began the dinner grace. "Dear God, thank you for this food and thank you for keeping our family together during this time of need. Also please protect Andrew's family in their underground fallout shelter in upstate New York. Please give us all strength and comfort, AMEN.

"Amen," was the closing, emitted in unison, from all of us at the table.

"What is going on out there?" we all simultaneously began asking John.

Since he had been on the shortwave radio all day giving directives and communicating with other militia cells, we felt he would probably be well versed on what the heck was going on.

"It seems that every country that ever had a complaint against the United States in the past one hundred years has joined in this massive buildup against us. A few additional countries like France and Italy, who have always joined the perceived *'winning team'*, have aligned themselves against us once again, as well," John stated, addressing our urgent need for information. "From the shortwave radio communications I've had, it appears that the first wave of the attack hit us by completely annihilating New York City, Washington, D.C., and San Francisco with both nuclear missiles and H-bombs."

"How the **hell** did they get close enough?! --Oh, sorry Mom," was Dan's quick response as his mother quickly gave him a curt look in response to his use of coarse language in front of her and the children.

"How the *heck* did they get close enough to bomb those major cities? Our military should have been all over them," said Dan in more acceptable English.

"That's what I thought," responded John. "It turns out, that this major attack has been planned for many years. You know all those battle skirmishes involving Iraq, Iran, Egypt, Saudi Arabia, Turkey, Syria, Lebanon, Pakistan, Palestine, Afghanistan, India, France, Ireland, Czech Republic, Sarajevo, North Korea, Singapore, China, and Japan that have consumed our U.N. Forces and Military for the past three months?"

"Yea," said Dan.

"Well it is feared that most of those skirmishes were simply ploys to draw our military away from our shores. As our military extended itself to help those in need abroad, we left ourselves more vulnerable here in the states."

"No way," Jim retorted. "Our military is too vast and sophisticated to be decoyed and set up like that."

"That's what I thought," responded John, "but one of the things that the enemy used to catch us off guard was a diversion of unparalleled magnitude. They nuked one of our carriers at 0100 EST, which drew one of our key remaining U.S.-stationed battle groups, including two killer-attack nuclear submarines, toward the Gulf of Oman to help stabilize the region and eventually initiate retaliatory measures. As that battle group was decoyed in from the Yokosuka, Japan area, another fleet, from our Pacific Coast, was sent in for backup. While those two U.S. Carrier Battle Groups (CVBG) were decoyed toward the Middle East, many of our other CVBG's were already engaged in addressing skirmishes throughout Europe. With the U.S. now overextending its Navy abroad, the enemy launched an attack against our shores. New York City, Washington, D.C., and San Francisco were their immediate targets, and they attacked those sites using large oil barges bearing nuclear missiles on their decks. Simple tarpaulins had hid the missile launchers and control consoles from view. Oil tankers have tarped their decks before to protect various import objects over the years, so our military surveillance and defense operatives had no reason to suspect them. They've gotten so used to seeing the tarps in the past that they never thought to check them this morning, especially with our attention then focused abroad. We let them navigate right up to our shores and nuke us. Enemy nuclear subs rushed in to further aid in the destruction of these three key communications and command cities resulting in political and military chaos. Lost at the New York City bombing were our U.N. and NATO headquarters. Killed in Washington were both the President of the United States and the Vice President, along with most of the Congressmen and Senate members. Both the Pentagon and our Washington-based Military Strategic Command Center were annihilated, severing U.S. military contact with these key agencies and people. This thing hit us with such surprise and severity that I doubt any of our leaders had a chance of survival. I am not yet certain why they nuked San Francisco, except perhaps to add to our chaos and further cut off communications between the states. We're now playing catch up, as enemy battle groups and killer-attack submarines are reaching our shores and lobbing nuclear-guided missiles into our coastal defense airfields from all three of our U.S. ocean coasts. Our overseas battle groups and military divisions are returning home. But ironically, in too many instances, we are following the enemy to our shores as opposed to intercepting them. Bombers dispatched from Cuba, and escorted by Russian made-fighter jets, succeeded in dropping an H-bomb on Washington to further ensure complete annihilation of that city."

"Wait a minute," Jim interjected, "you're overwhelming me with data that doesn't make rational sense. Number one, --was it a Lexington II-Class Navy Carrier they bombed?"

"Yep," responded John.

"That's impossible," Jim exclaimed. "Those things are always part of a full battle group, which makes them indestructible."

"Virtually indestructible," corrected John.

"What's going to happen now?" interrupted John's elderly mother.

As I looked over to John's mother, she appeared approximately eighty-five years of age, frail, and terrified. As I watched her pitiful expressions of utmost concern manifest themselves, I became sympathetic to her fears, and I worried about her health under such pressure.

John stated that she would be able to continue her life in the farmhouse, as usual, unless the war came to our area.

"If the enemy or radiation fallout reaches our area," he said, "we will all need to retreat to the fallout shelter. You will be safe there, Mom," stated John reassuringly.

"And we will take good care of you," John's wife, Sharon added. "Everything is prepared down there for an extended stay, if warranted."

With these words I began mentally counting those at the table, discretely using my eyes, without turning my head.

One: John Cindrich

Two: John's wife, Sharon

Three: John's daughter, Debbie, of six years

Four: John's son, Michael of three years

Five: Dan Cindrich

Six: Dan Cindrich's wife, Susan

Seven: Jim Fletcher

Eight: John's mother, approximately eighty-five years old

Nine: John's mother's live in-aid, Mrs. Long, sixty-eight years old.

Ten: Me

"Oh brother," I thought. "If we all have to fit into that bunker for an extended period of time, it's going to be sheer hell. I'll bet Carol and Kelly have the same overcrowded and cramped situation at their Clawson, NY bunker and they are already stuck in that thing in order to avoid the nuclear fallout from the New York City bombing. Boy, I feel sorry for them. I wish I was there to be with them," I thought in earnest.

Jim interrupts my reflections with a loud question poised to John, while John is seen finishing his last bite of pot roast. "What is the current status of the invasion?"

I interrupted, "what's a battle group?" I asked. "And what's a 'Lexington II'?" I quickly added.

As all eyes turned to my person in scorn for interrupting this increasingly intense conversation between knowledgeable ex-military men, I realized that I was out of my league and elected to excuse myself from the table and find something productive to do with my time. I joined the children in the next room, who had already exercised the intelligence to disperse and leave the dining room to these military men. As I entered the living room with the kids, they were already busy in the far corner of the room playing with some small board games. The children's mother and grandmother soon joined us, and were welcome company to both my person and damaged ego. Dan's wife remained in the dining room, with the ex-military men, since she was an honorably discharged ex-Marine nurse who understood their lingo and contributed to their conversation.

John's wife, who seated herself to the far end of the sofa from me, was also ex-military. She had joined the Army out of high school, and had met John at one of their off- base college classes at the Fort Drum Army Base in Watertown, New York. She immediately became attracted to him since they shared many common backgrounds. Though surprisingly from the same hometown of Wellsville, Ohio they had never known one another since their age difference of three years was enough to cast them into different social circles while in high school. At college, their souls seemed destined for uniting, until John was called to active duty in Vietnam. Sharon would not see him again until his return to Wellsville three years hence. There was a reunion of tears and sorrow, rather than rapture. They had both been witnesses to a terrible war that had changed them acutely.

Sharon took the role of unassuming nurturer to John's now tormented soul, while he relished the bliss he found in the distractions that she offered him from his devastatingly painful memories of Vietnam. They were married within a year's time and the uniting of their two souls brought them both back to our world as whole beings once again. Beings who could again take pleasure in a life that, without their union, would be dark and bleak, and perhaps, even unworthy of continuance. I know of these facts from prior conversations with John at his office and it was a pleasure and honor to now have his wife, this precious spirit, joining me in conversation.

As Sharon watched the children, I began asking the many questions I sensed she already knew I needed to ask.

"Sharon, what is a 'Lexington II'?"

"Well," she responded while the children calmly played with games at the far corner of the room and 'Grandma' sat rocking near the warmth of the large, stone fireplace, "it's a....." Then, before she continued, Sharon covered her mouth with one hand, and attempted to hold back laughter. "Andrew," she began again, "I must first apologize for chuckling slightly, but you don't have a clue about military terminology do you?"

"No Ma'am," I responded jokingly, using one of the few military addresses I knew and then laughing to break the ice.

"Sharon, I've been fortunate to never be in war, nor was I ever in the ROTC or any other military organization. I don't have a clue about what those guys in the other room are talking about. I don't even know how to tell military time.

It's ironic that I am this ignorant of military matters or terminology since my maternal grandfather was a marksman in WWI, my father was a Marine on Iwo Jima, my uncle William was a military attaché to a top U.S. military officer stationed in Russia, my uncle John was a WWII fighter pilot, and my older brother Raymond was drafted into the Vietnam war. Throughout a lifetime of exposure to all those military people around me, you'd have thought that I would have been privy to military terminology, but they never talked about their war experiences around me, nor to anyone I know of. When asked about the war, each would change the subject and I quickly sensed, in youth, that these were questions to avoid. I did not learn that my dad had been pushed through three full Marine platoons during the invasion of Iwo Jima until after his death in 1985. My uncle had told me the story as we reminisced after the burial. My dad died at age 64 of a massive heart attack due to years of overwork and high anxiety. After the funeral, my uncle had told me that; as the members of one of my dad's platoon's were annihilated by enemy fire, my dad would be absorbed into the next wave of fighters and become part of their forward momentum into enemy fire. After thirty-six days of fighting, and after witnessing the deaths of his comrades from three full-platoons, he was certain that my dad could have told me all the details I wanted to know about war, but had elected not to. His reasons, I remember thinking, though undiscernible in youth, were at that time all too transparent. He and my other relatives, who had been thrown in the pits of the darkest hell that war can bring, emerged so severely shaken from their experiences that they had to keep their minds from returning to those dreaded places of Hades. The alternative would be to lose their minds to those dark and hellish places their bodies had long ago escaped.

Simply put, Sharon, I don't know a darn thing about war or the military and, if it wasn't for your husband's aid, my family and I would be helpless and in grave peril."

"Let's start with the Lexington II," Sharon interjected. "I think we're going to have plenty of time to talk, as we hold up here over the next few weeks, so we might as well start now with your crash course in military education."

"A Lexington II-Class Aircraft Carrier is a 4.8-billion dollar, 100,000-ton warship that spans 332 meters in length and stands twenty-four stories high from her keel to her masthead," begins Sharon with the vocal command of a new-recruit orientation instructor. "This vessel carries slightly over six thousand men, including six hundred of the Navy's best-trained officers, on a total of ten horizontal decks. Two nuclear reactors power her, and each of her four prop drive shafts is about the length and thickness of a hundred-year-old giant California redwood tree.

Her belly, continued Sharon, contains eighty mach-one fighter/attack aircraft in hangars the size of three football fields. The ship is laden with millions of gallons of aircraft fuel, her own fuel reservoirs, entire batteries of artillery and guns, and missiles capable of carrying nuclear warheads."

"Well, no wonder our carrier was bombed in the strait. It's so large that it would be an easy target for any enemy force," I replied.

"It's not as easy to attack a U.S. carrier as you might think. This ship doesn't travel alone. It is defended with a huge armada of ships called a Carrier Vessel Battle Group or CVBG. The battle group consists of two hunter-killer nuclear submarines to protect her from underwater attack. Above the water line, the flotilla includes destroyers, computer-guided-missile cruisers, and frigates. She also has a sophisticated system of surveillance radar from outer space, and other ships, that enable her to detect an enemy approaching from over a thousand miles out.

With all of her technical abilities and firepower, no one would ever think it possible to sink her. But, whichever country destroyed this ship today not only sunk her, they nuked her atoms to kingdom come; double hull and all."

"Why do they call it a 'Lexington II'?" I asked.

"The Lexington I aircraft carrier, was sunk in the Battle of Coral Sea on May 8, 1942. Lexington II was named in honor of Lexington I, during its christening ceremony conducted by Ronald Reagan in 1984."

"Thanks to the Reagan administration, we had an up-to-date carrier available to send to the Gulf," I added while adjusting to a more comfortable sitting position on the couch.

"I believe the Lexington probably first received its name as a reference to the U.S. militia skirmish in Lexington, MA in 1775 against British soldiers," Sharon added as I got comfortable again.

"Time for bed," interrupted John with his booming voice, as he and his military entourage entered our room from the dining room. "We've got a long night ahead of us and an early morning to rise to. Jim will take the first watch of the perimeter for possible enemy intruders, and he'll also periodically monitor the air for possible increased radiation levels. Dan will man the shortwave transceiver, and the rest of us need to hit the sack. Andrew, I'll need you to relieve Jim at 0300 hours, and I will relieve Dan at the same time."

"That's no problem John, but what the heck is 0300 hours?" I queried.

"Three A.M.," he quipped. "Now everyone to bed, please."

As I passed him on my way upstairs to the room, that was previously designated as Jim's and my bedroom, John stopped me and talked in a low whisper.

"When we start our shifts, I'll see if we can reach your family via voice."

"Great," I responded.

"Good night."

"Good night, Colonel," I responded, as I reeled back around to face him and saluted. As I quickly turned and headed for bed, I could see John smile and shake his head in comical disbelief.

"Good night you asshole," he responded without realizing that his mother was being helped to her bedroom by Mrs. Long, and they were both standing right behind him.

As she cleared her throat in reprimand, John turned with a start to face her.

"Oh, sorry mom."

"Being separated from one's daughter in her time of need, is the worst of feelings that can beset a man."

Andrew Henry's diary dated February 21, 2004. Entered during his second morning at the bomb shelter between the hours of 2:30 A.M.and 3:45 A.M. He was 49 years of age at the time of this entry.

Chapter Ten: Watch at 0300

No sooner did my exhausted head hit my pillow then, it seemed, I was rudely awakened by my 2:30 A.M. alarm. I reluctantly left my warm bed to shower and prepare for my seven-hour shift at watch. "I don't believe this is happening." I thought. "We are actually being invaded and my poor wife and daughter are stranded in a dark, probably cold, underground bomb shelter in upstate New York. -- Boy, I sure hope we get out of this mess soon."

As I walked downstairs and out onto the front porch, the moonbeams, emanating from behind the house, illuminated the front yard and Ohio river before me. As I peered through the early morning mist, toward the road and the Ohio River beyond, I saw Jim walking toward me from the corner of my right eye.

"Ya ready to feed the chickens?" was my comment to Jim, as he slowly walked up to the front porch.

"No," was his response. "But I am ready for bed. From the far side of the road over there, you can look down on the Ohio River about five kilometers out and see the Eastern Horizon. Check for boats on the river or any incoming attack aircraft.

"How will I know if they're attack aircraft or our own?"

"Any enemy attack aircraft will be coming at us from the east, and they'll probably be in some type of group formation. I've seen some of our own fighters, bombers, and C-130's, but they're all flying to the east, and most are not returning. Those that are returning, are solitary planes with no escorts. If they ever start coming this far inland, the enemy will come as a large formation of planes."

(Source: A sketch by Andrew Henry, from his personal diary dated 1998-2004).

"What's a C-130?" I asked Jim as he walked past me toward the door.

"It's a heavy cargo and personnel carrier. They are huge and brown, or camouflage color. When they fly overhead, they are so immense, they look like they're hoverin' rather than flyin', but they're traveling between 200 and 300 knots. Anyway, I've got to get to bed. Let John know if you see anything."

"Okay."

"See ya' at 1000."

"What?"

"10:00 A.M."

Boy, I felt stupid as Jim entered the house and left me alone in the stillness of this brisk February morning. A light snow had fallen, in the night, and about two centimeters covered everything. As I walked out to check out the Ohio River and the Eastern Horizon, I saw John entering the barn. I quickly summarized that he was going to relieve Dan at the shortwave radio post.

"Oh, that's right," I thought. "If atmospheric conditions are favorable, John's going to try to reach my family by voice."

I hurried my pace to check out the east, as instructed, and finding everything peaceful, with no enemy intruders heading our way, I quickly circled back to the barn. I knew that John would now be in the fallout shelter relieving Dan of his ham radio duty, and I was anxious to see if we could contact my family. As I entered the shelter, Dan and John were talking about the night's events.

"Oh, and I found out more information about that Lexington II-Class Aircraft Carrier that was bombed," Dan said. It appears that the carrier, and its flotilla, was heading down the Strait of Hormuz toward the Persian Gulf, when they were attacked at the bend. Just as they entered that area of the strait where it bends along at Abbas, Iran, they were decoyed by an attack against one of their destroyers by some Russian-built fighters. As customary, our carrier had to launch its fighters into the wind, so while it slowly maneuvered into launch position, it was hit from both shores of the strait by missiles armed with who-knows-how-many nuclear warheads. While it listed in the water, a bomber immediately flew overhead guarded by an entire squadron of Iranian fighter jets, and they dropped an H-bomb on it. No one knows what happened to the bomber or the escort jets, but preliminary news reports suggest it was a suicide mission. They were flying way too low to have survived the blast." "How did you find all this out?" asked John.

"It was on *the BBC* radio broadcast I picked up at 2400. They're still at 5.975 MHz and, *The Voice of America* is still active, just slightly up the dial at 6.035 MHz. Hell, I even brought in *Radio Austria International* at 6.015 MHz.

"What brought them into the strait in the first place? They knew that was a hot zone."

"Kuwait was being heavily shelled by an Iranian battleship, and our battle group was called in to help".

"I didn't think Iran had battleships," I interjected.

"Oh, boy! That's a sore subject with John and me," exclaimed Dan. "Since Ronald Reagan was President, our past and current Presidents, along with Congress, have been dismantling the U.S. military and cutting back its resources. At the same time, our adversaries have been investing heavily in military armament and nuclear-bomb technology. John and I have always been pissed-off that the American people became so damned apathetic, civilized, naive, and supercilious that they decided to ignore the barbaric and tyrannous world around them."

"We're like the Greek, the Roman, the Babylonian, and the Egyptian empires," added Jim. "All of these civilizations were conquered by more aggressive countries after becoming so accustomed to peace, that they let down their guard. At that time, they were annihilated. Civilized people always seem to forget that there will always be a spirit of both good and evil on this earth. Whenever evil is given the opportunity to triumph, it will seize the chance. We've let down our guard, and now every country with a past grudge against us sees this as payback time."

"We're viewed," said John, "as a sophisticated, peace-loving people by our citizenry, while many other countries view us as the evil empire inflicting our will on their people. They've been building up for this day for two decades now while, at the same time, the U.S. has been cutting back. This is going to be one hell of a war. In our eyes they are the evil forces, but in their eyes we are the evil aggressors who must be conquered before we encroach even further on their lands and the will of their people. All wars are based on evil thoughts propagated by evil men. The victors of those wars have always been the military forces that are best prepared for battle. In relationship to empirical proportions, our military is at the greatest disadvantage it has ever been in the last century. We have depleted our forces to an alarming level and our technology is no longer completely superior to the enemies. It is technology that wins wars, not a soldier's effort or ending death count. Hiroshima and Nagasaki serve as constant reminders of that truism."

"Anyway," Dan said, continuing our previous conversation, "when our battle group, stationed in the Gulf of Oman, was called into the aid of the Kuwaitis, they focused on the battle they expected in the Persian Gulf and probably let are guard down slightly while in the strait."

"Who launched the missiles?" queried John.

"It appears from initial reports that there was an oil tanker moored on each shore. They had missile launchers mounted on their decks with simple brown tarps as camouflage. When our aircraft carrier stopped to position its deck into the wind for the launching of its fighter aircraft, enemy military crews hiding in the oil tanker's belly, stormed onto their decks, uncovered their missile launchers, took aim, and shot. That diversion sent more of our attention to that region, while the enemy assault on the U.S. began."

"Holy cow," John exclaimed. "You mean to tell me that they had thought out a series of diversions before attacking our shores?"

"You got it," rattled Jim.

"Their timing and planning were perfectly instrumented," retorted John. "We're not dealing with the unsophisticated militaries of the past. These guys have learned how to fight and strategize."

"I know I'm ignorant of these things," I interrupted, "but wouldn't an H- Bomb have sunk the other boats escorting the Carrier as well as its two or three escort nuclear subs? And those oil tankers would have been incinerated in the blast as well, wouldn't they?"

"Very good Andrew, you're catching on."

"What about it?" inquired John to Dan.

Dan replied saying, "According to the BBC report, there was a massive tidal wave after the bombing that demolished all buildings on both shores and grounded those ships and subs that survived the initial blast. They didn't have more details at this time, but the entire battle group is out of commission. We learned about the tankers during a news conference given by the now gloating President of Iran. He told his people that; 'the Jihad against the United States has begun', or something to that effect."

"These daw-gone' Iranians are on a holy crusade," interrupted John. "They don't care about themselves or anyone else. They feel that their deaths as martyrs to their Islamic Holy War against Jews, Christians, and the United States imperialists, as they call us, will ensure their place in heaven with Mohammed and God. They want vengeance for our past transgressions against them, and their recent acquisitions of nuclear technology will allow them to exact it."

"Shit," Dan interjected with a thoughtful expression on his face as he rubbed his chin with his right hand. "Just think of the effect that H-bomb blast had on our aircraft carrier and respective flotilla. That one hydrogen bomb would have probably been even more powerful than the atomic bomb we dropped on Hiroshima, Japan during World War II. The initial explosion in Hiroshima killed approximately 100,000 people within a 3.5-kilometer radius from the bomb's hypocenter and an additional 40,000 people died shortly after due to severe radiation exposure.

The temperature of the initial fireball was over 100,000° C and people near the center of the blast were completely incinerated. Investigators and health care workers witnessed char marks the shape of people on a few concrete sidewalks, with no human remains. One investigator was noted as saying that what he thought was a chalk outline of a corpse left by investigators had turned out to be the victim's ash marks. The victim's form had been burned into the concrete by the severe heat of the initial blast. Other reports from investigators told of survivors walking from wreckage with their skin burned off their bodies and dropping down in flaps. One hundred percent of those receiving these severe thermal burns from exposure within one kilometer of the hypocenter, without shielding, died within a week. People were reported to have been literally blown far away by the blast causing fatal injuries."

"So the Iranians not only annihilated the military men in command of our battle group, they also killed thousands of civilians on each side of the strait?" queried John.

"Oh, yea," said Dan. "But what's worse is the pain they've inflicted on their own people for the next sixty years. The survivors of Hiroshima suffered radiation sickness and death from radiation exposure for many decades after the explosion. Some are still suffering. The immediate radiation sickness symptoms were nausea, vomiting, excessive thirst, loss of appetite, and fever. Later the victim's hair would begin to fall out and nasal bleeding and gingival hemorrhage would often occur. In later years, leukemia and cancerous malignancies took their toll on survivors who had been exposed to high doses of radiation exceeding the two-hundred-rad level. These high levels of radiation had caused injury to red blood cells, white blood cells, and platelets."

"Those poor civilians over there don't have a chance," lamented John.

"John, could we call my wife and daughter tonight?"

"Oh yea! No problem," responded John. "Dan, go get some sleep and thanks for the report. I'll see you back here at 1000."

"Yes, Sir," responded Dan with a salute timed with his turning toward the door on his heels.

John chuckled and said, "You're getting as bad as Andrew."

Dan laughed and yelled back, "See ya' later brother!"

John began meticulously tuning the dial of his radio and verbally searching for contact with his Logan, N.Y. militia cell; --the cell that now protected my wife and daughter in their bunker. We couldn't contact them directly, but were able to do so via a relay.

The relay was another Ham Radio operator in Rochester, N.Y. From his position he could reach my family's bunker, so we relayed our transmissions through him.

"How's the war going where you are?" inquired Colonel Cindrich of Lieutenant White.

"We're all hunkered down until this radioactive plume blows over, and the low winds are taking their time getting it out of here."

"How are our military troops doing?" inquired John.

"They are fighting despite the radioactive fallout. But there is so much chaos no one knows how we're doing, yet. The enemy has taken a few of our coastal airfields and they're severing as many communications lines as they can. They're also destroying as many of our power plants as they can. And regarding the nuclear power plants they're blowing up, well hell, --that's not helping our radioactive fallout problem."

It seemed eerie that this voice was not the actual voice of Lieutenant White, but actually the voice of Sam Thompson of Rochester, N.Y. simply relaying information by voice for us.

"The damned interesting thing," responded Lieutenant White, (through our relayer Sam), "is that some other ham radio operators are reporting something that scares the hell out of me. They say that just prior to the attacks on New York City, Washington, and San Francisco all the computers went down, along with telephones and electric power. We can't figure out how the enemy did it, but they were able to create a severe electromagnetic disturbance before launching their missiles from sea. Who knows, since they seem to have just about everybody on their side, maybe the Martians are helping them as well."

"Was the disturbance isolated to just those cities?"

"Yep," retorted Lieutenant White. "Seemed like it was limited to a two-kilometer radius. I know you can wipe out computer disks, digital data, and affect power using a heavy-duty magnet, but if they sent a magnetic wave from a space satellite it would have moved light metal objects and scattered all kinds of light debris. --It didn't. --It just screwed up communications and computers and created chaos a few minutes before the missiles hit. We don't have any idea of the technology the enemy is using, but neither did the Japs at Hiroshima and Nagasaki when we hit them with our A-Bombs."

"Lieutenant," interrupted Dan, "Carol Henry's husband is with me and he would like to talk to his wife and daughter."

"Roger, Sir! Here they are."

"Hi Andrew," came Carol's welcomed greeting.

Finally talking with her was wonderful, but being forced to relay our words through Sam Thompson, the Ham Radio operator in Rochester, diluted the effect.

"Sorry we can't talk directly, but John says the ionosphere limits direct communication with his type of ham radio tonight. --How are you doing?"

"Terrible, but at least we're alive. I feel awful for the twenty million people in the New York City and Long Island area who have lost their lives, but I feel even worse for those above ground who are out in this radioactive fallout with no radioactive fallout shelter to retreat to."

"I know, I feel terrible for all of you. The war hasn't hit us yet in Ohio, but the torment I feel being separated from you and Kelly is worse than death. As soon as you two can get out into the open again, call me and I'll come out to immediately join you."

"Okay, we will. Here's Kelly. I love you very much. Good-bye and take care."

"I love you too."

"Hi Dad!" Even though Kelly's voice was being relayed by Sam Thompson's voice, I could sense its true sound. I had heard it many times before, over many years of long-distance phone calls to home, while on the road as salesman.

"Hi, Kelly." was my response. "Sorry to wake you up, but we won't be able to reach you verbally during the day."

"That's okay. When are you going to be here?"

"As soon as that radioactive cloud above you blows over. It should only be a day or two."

"I'm scared," was Kelly's reply.

"She's crying now," interjected Sam's relay voice as he immediately ceased being a strict translator and changed into a more human intermediary.

"Tell her it will be okay, Sam"

"Your dad says it will be okay. He will be there in a few days."

"The militiamen who got us at our house said that we had to let Ben and Abbey loose to fend for themselves. They even made me let Missy go."

"Sam," I said, "Ben and Abbey are our dogs, and Missy is our daughter's cat."

"Won't the radiation make them sick and die?" asked Kelly.

"Not if it's not strong enough. If it blows over soon, they'll be all right. They are probably waiting right at our house for you as we speak. When you guys are able to get out of your shelter, you can go home and take care of them again. --Don't worry."

"Tell her I love her."

"Your dad say he loves you."

"Bye, Dad. Hurry home!"

"I will, Kelly. I hope to be there in two days. --Bye, I love you."

-End of transmission.-

I sat there staring at the bench across the shelter with tears running down my cheeks as John signed off the radio. I was raised not to cry by a tough ex-Marine, but I guess war and separation from loved-ones brings out our strongest feelings.

"Home and family render shelter from a tumultuous sea of despair."

Andrew Henry's diary dated February 21, 2004 at 10: 45 A.M.

Chapter Eleven: At Last, -- Homeward Bound

It was 10:00 A.M. and Jim was now relieving me of my watch. As I looked out to the Eastern Horizon the sun shone brightly and everything looked deceptively normal and peaceful. It was at this moment that I knew it was time to depart for home, --radiation or no radiation. At worst, I thought, I may develop cancer several years down the road from radiation exposure, but that was an unimportant consideration when compared to my need to reunite with my wife and daughter. There is nothing more devastating to a soul, than to be needed by your family and not be able to be there for them. I must go, and I must go now!

After quickly packing my toiletry items from my bedroom, I said my good-byes to all in the house and bolted out the front door. Upon hitting the bottom step on the porch, I saw John coming out of the barn. We met halfway between the house and barn to say our good-byes.

"Thanks for everything John, but now that my watch is over I've got to get home, whether the radiation levels are high or not."

"Andrew," John said. "I have bad news." "Your wife and daughter were killed. --I just found out about it via my radio five minutes ago. I'm very sorry."

"What!?" I exclaimed. "They couldn't have been killed 'cause they were protected by the fallout shelter."

"It wasn't the radiation plume that killed them. That blew over early this morning. It was the enemy forces. They found the fallout shelter and killed all inside as part of their scorch and burn campaign. Members of a neighboring militia cell group found their bodies in the shelter. All twelve people were killed, including your wife and daughter."

"How do they know it was my wife and daughter?" I immediately asked.

"You know Dick Cunningham who works in Stonewall, New York don't you?"

"Yes," I responded.

"He knows your wife and daughter and identified their bodies."

I turned from John and walked slowly down to the mound across the road overlooking the Ohio. I sat and profusely, intensely, and inappropriately cursed God with a string of impulsive and violent expletives for what seemed like several minutes. --Then I wept.

"Andrew get up to the house now!" screamed John from a position immediately behind me.

"What?" I questioned while still half in a daze and totally disgusted with his request.

"Fighter jets just flew over Pittsburgh, and they'll be overhead any minute now. We need to get my entire family into the shelter, and NOW!

"No! --Go screw yourself," was my reply. "I don't care if the enemy attacks! I don't care IF I GET RADIATION SICKNESS. I DON'T GIVE A DAMN IF OUR ENTIRE GOD FORESAKEN WORLD BLOWS UP. Get outa' here!" I began screaming at John. "Get outa' here! --I don't care if those murdering legions of demented demons come flying right over my head. I JUST DON'T CARE ANYMORE! GO AND LEAVE ME ALONE. --GO!"

John took off to the house in a full run, but I was certain it was not as a result of my verbal assault but rather to save his family from a rapidly intruding enemy force. I remained at my perch atop the mound, along the far side of the road, for another five minutes or so. I reflected on my plight while staring into the vast Ohio River below. As the planes approached, I could see a large plane in the center like the Ohio National Guard cargo planes I was accustomed to seeing while living in Decorah, Ohio. Around this large plane was a "V" formation of fighter jets. There was no way that I could tell what country they were from since they were too far away for me to see their insignias. More importantly, I thought, I could not discern what they meant even if I did see them. --I've never been exposed to the insignias of other countries. The only ones I know are the Japanese insignias from the many war movies I watched as a child and the Nazi swastika that you still see today as a graffiti mark designed to invoke rage on its viewer.

I don't give a spit if those fowl heathens shoot me right here on this knoll, I thought, as they continued to fly to me. I could hear their mighty engines coming closer and closer and closer. I could see their planes becoming larger and larger and larger. And I could even see the silhouettes of the fighter pilots in their cockpits as the lead planes turned directly over the Ohio River and began flying down river. At the moment that the large plane in the center of the

(Source: A sketch by Andrew Henry, from his personal diary dated 1998-2004).

formation turned south, heading down river, the door on its side opened. Someone peered out and seemed to look directly at me. And then, with a wave of his hand as a signal, paratroopers began tumbling out. It looked like a scene out of Kevin Reynold's old movie *"Red Dawn"* as their camouflaged chutes opened. I remembered thinking that it was odd that they were camouflaged in color as opposed to white like those in the many war movies I had watched in my youth. It was ridiculous that I would think such a mundane thought during this time of crisis, but it always seems funny how your mind addresses crisis in a slow and calculating manner. It's as if the entire world around you is moving in slow motion, and you have all the time in the world to think about superfluous things. As I snapped out of my daze, while looking up at the invading paratroopers,

I remember not being able to believe that those fiends who were indirectly responsible for my wife and daughter's slaughter, possessed the audacity to land at my feet.

With this thought, I went crazy and started running towards my car for my pistol. I grabbed my .25 caliber handgun out of the bag that I always carry it in, and began running back down the bank toward the Ohio River as fast as I could. As I reached the west bank of the river, there were paratroopers landing all over in the muddy riverbank and into the thickets and scrub brush along the shore. I saw one soldier in the water struggling to control his shoot and get to shore. I walked into the water to my waist and shot the infiltrating scum, emptying my pistol into his body. I then swam out to grab his pistol since mine was now out of ammunition. As I was just about to reach the corpse three bullets splashed in the water around me. I submerged myself and swam underwater surfacing slowly on the far side of the dead, floating soldier. I could not see anything from my position, but I could at least breathe. The floating body, separating me from the sight of the soldiers on the bank, was hiding my head which was sticking slightly out of the water. After lying there motionless and floating with the corpse for what seemed like an eternity in the frigid water, I finally began searching his waistline for his pistol. I could not find a pistol on his belt, so I began groping about his ankles while remaining as inconspicuous as possible from the enemy on shore. Around his left ankle I found a large, five-inch, knife but no pistol. I removed the knife from it sheath.

After lying motionless for a few more minutes I could see, by discretely looking downstream, that the paratroopers were now running down-river toward the power plant. Perhaps it would be safe, I thought, to peer up over the corpse toward the shore immediately in front of me. As I slowly moved my drenched head over the body of the slain man, I could barely make out a thing. Being that it was February, the cold air had steamed up my wet glasses so I couldn't tell if an enemy soldier was, at this very moment, about to shoot me in the head or not. I was afraid to move my head again out of fear of being discovered, yet, at the same time, was also reluctant to leave it in its current exposed position for fear a rifle bullet would be piercing my forehead at any minute. With that uneasy thought, I quickly returned my head back to the water level on the far side of my victim.

"Damn," I thought, as I shivered alongside the corpse. My hands and body were now cramping from the ice-cold water and my hyperventilation noises were growing louder at an uncontrollable pace. I stuck my head back into the water to clear the cursed steam from my glasses while holding onto the corpse with both hands. I then pulled myself up so I could again examine the shore. As I cautiously peered over the top to the corpse, I scanned the shoreline discretely by moving my eyes from side to side. --I saw nothing.

I then rotated my head to look upstream and then downstream. --Nothing. No soldiers were in view. They all seemed to have landed and run toward the power plant. There appeared to have been about a dozen that had landed which meant there were only eleven left for us to kill, "now that this bastard's dead", I thought.

I immediately dunked my entire body under the water again, swimming under my victim and up to shore. As I surfaced, I was prepared to feel a bullet pierce my body, but was fortunate to have surfaced and exposed myself, unharmed. I walked up the slippery mud bank, pulling myself out of the frigid water by grabbing onto those thin red bushes (Red Osier Dogwood/Cornus Sericea) that seem to grow on every stream bank in America. Upon hoisting myself safely to solid ground again, I ran back up the hill to the farmhouse, hyperventilating the entire way due to the cold river water that drenched my clothes. As I ran, the hairs on my head fused together in a stiff and frozen mat. Upon reaching the farm house I bolted into the front door, ran upstairs, and quickly undressed and dried off. After warming my frigid and shaking body by the bedroom wood stove, I dressed into some of Mrs. Cindrich's deceased husband's clothes and searched the house for a shotgun or a rifle.

I found a shotgun in a gun rack located in the living room and found the ammunition that I needed in an adjoining drawer. I quickly loaded the chamber only to find that it would only take three shells. "Damn," I muttered, as I quickly ejected the three shells I had just loaded, "They've got a plug in it." A plug is used by duck and geese hunters. It ensures that only three shells can be inserted into the gun at one time. One more government rule screwing me up, I thought as I took the gun to the kitchen to remove the plug. Using a quarter from the kitchen drawer, I unscrewed the screw holding the chamber where the wooden 'plug' lay. I removed the plug and then quickly reloaded the gun with six twelve-gauge shells. I then ran out the front door, down the front steps, and through the barn to the shelter.

"John, it's me. Let me in," I yelled when I had found the shelter door closed and surmized that John and his family were inside. The door opened, and I burst into the room with emotion.

"John," I exclaimed, "did you see 'em?"

"Yea, we saw them, and we also saw you go running after them like a maniac."

"Those hell-demons killed my family, and they're gonna' pay."

"Well that's great for you Andrew, but Dan and my family are still alive and we've got to protect them."

"John," replied Sharon. "You guys can go. We'll be all right, and we can take care of the kids and grandma, without you here. --You, Dan, and Jim have trained for this day all your lives. Now go and do whatever you can to help hinder this attack against the U.S."

"Okay Sharon," you're right, responded John. "Dan, you stay here and continue to using the transceiver to coordinate communications with our other militia cells in the area. We'll go down to the river and try to figure out what these guys are up to. We'll keep you informed of our findings so that you can notify our regular military forces."

"We'll be back once we've figured out what they're up to."

"Love ya!" were John's final words as he quickly kissed his wife, two children, and mother on the way out the door.

After John, Jim, and I left the shelter we could hear Dan's wife Susan shut the shelter door behind us. The three of us ran through the barn to the outside, then quickly down to road where we headed south, parallel to the river. As we ran down the road, I quickly took to the relaxed stride I had learned during my days as a high-school cross-country and long-distance runner. I noticed that John and Jim were running with the same well-paced and relaxed stride that I presume they learned during their days in basic training, and then afterward, during their regular militia training exercises.

For a bunch of over-forty men, we were moving along quite readily. Their quick cadence, devoid of heavy breathing, could be attributed to years of training in the cases of John and Jim; while my quick cadence, allowing me to keep pace with them, was derived by a mind set upon revenge. My normal bodily aches and pains were gone and I was with one purpose only, --revenge. And if I was killed while inflicting that revenge, all the better, for then I could be reunited with my family providing there is a heaven waiting for us in death. And if there is nothing after death save the grave, then I would rather be dead than spend my remaining days on earth, remorseful and guilty for not having saved my family from these invading heathens.

"Stop," John whispered as he immediately held up his hand as a signal for us to stop.

"They're down there at the nuclear power plant."

The power plant was located along the Ohio River about halfway between John's mother's farmhouse and the hunting lean-to we stayed at back in November.

"Let's slowly sneak down the bank so that we can figure out what they're up to."

Before we could get to an observation position, we heard a series of three sets of machinegun fire. When we got close enough to see the power plant, we could finally discern what the shooting was for. There were about thirty-five power plant workers lying dead in front of the entrance wall of the plant. They must have been led out of the building and killed in firing-squad fashion by those bastards. Their still bodies could be clearly seen with John's binoculars as they lay at the bottom of the hill less than a half- kilometer away from our position.

"What the hell," Jim whispered to John.

"It must be the plutonium and uranium they're after."

"Why would they want that?" I whispered.

Continuing in low, hushed, voice, John explained, "the uranium used to fuel the plant could be used to make nuclear warheads. The plutonium residue generated from the nuclear reactor could also be used for the same diabolical purposes. A sphere of plutonium the size of a baseball can produce an explosion equaling 20,000 tons of TNT when hooked up properly in a warhead or bomb. The way they're attacking us with massive nuclear weapons, the enemy knows it will need more of these key substances for the manufacture of more bombs."

"Look at those guys coming out with silver suits and gas masks," Jim said.

"That confirms it. They want to secure our nuclear power plants and manufacture or take out the plutonium and uranium respectively. Let's get back to the radio and notify the regular military of our findings."

"Bang!" A gun went off behind us, and John immediately fell forward onto his face. As I whirled around with my shotgun aimed at our assailant, Jim sprang to the left and began running toward the enemy soldier who was standing only three meters behind us.

As I pushed the safely lever of my shotgun into the 'off' position, I could see in the enemy's eyes that he was about to squeeze his shot off before I could pull my trigger. Next I heard Jim's .45 caliber pistol go off to my left, and I saw the soldier's head jerk to the left side of his body as Jim's bullet entered the right side of his skull. I Immediately felt the pain of my assailant's bullet as it ripped through my left shoulder blade. I jerked my trigger as I fell backwards and saw the enemy soldier's head blow completely off, from my close range shotgun blast, before I hit the ground.

As I rolled off my back and rose again to a standing position, I turned to see if the other soldiers at the power plant were running up the hill toward us. They were, and that was no surprise. What was surprising was the sight of John pushing his face out of the ground and slowly standing back up on the side of the hill we were on. He turned to Jim and me and began pounding his chest like an idiot while smiling from ear-to-ear the entire time. It was a ghastly and unnatural sight since we felt for sure that he was dead. He was shot in the back at close range by a .45 caliber pistol. There is no way he could be standing and smiling, I thought.

"Bulletproof vest," he proclaimed. "Front and back. --I never leave home with out it."

"That's great," said Jim, "but let's get outa' here and now! We've got company coming."

As John turned to look down the hill where Jim and I were now looking, four soldiers, running two meters abreast of one another, were charging our position; -- and we fled.

As we ran down the road toward the farmhouse, I handed Jim my shotgun.

"Here, take this," I yelled to Jim while simultaneously handing him my gun.

As I ran, the pain in my left shoulder was astronomical. I could not swing my left arm to the rhythm of my stride, so it was difficult for me to keep up with Jim and John. As their distance from me increased, my stride slackened and I finally slowed to a walk. Then I simply sat down thinking that it didn't matter if I died. I deserved to die after having allowed my wife and daughter to be murdered without me at their side to help them. Besides, the excruciating pain in my left shoulder made it just too difficult to run.

As I sat waiting for the coming soldiers, I could see them nowhere. I peered down the road from my sitting position in the center of the road, and could ascertain no moving being. After five more minutes of squinting to see my expected liberators from life, I saw none. --They must have given up on us and returned to the power plant.

"Come on Andrew," was heard to my rear.

As I turned, I saw that John and Jim had run back down the road to give me a hand. I waved them on yelling. "Go back to the shelter. The soldiers gave up on us. --I'll join you in a while. --Hurry up and go now. I'll be all right."

They turned and began running down the road again towards the shelter where John's family awaited his return.

I simply sat there ascertaining the extent of the damage to my shoulder and lamenting about my predicament as I sat in the middle of a road, in a forest, eight hours away from home. After several minutes of reflection and self-criticism for loosing my family and getting shot, I stood up and began despairingly walking back to the shelter.

As I entered the farmhouse yard and continued walking to the barn, I could see a formation of five large attack helicopters coming toward my position. They were following the same flight path that the original intruding aircraft took. I sat down again in the open field to rest and to watch. As they approached, their engines became louder and louder. As they continued to approach their size became larger and larger. And as they reached the Ohio River, they turned downstream toward the power plant. They were low enough and close enough that I could see the pilots' helmets as they flew by, and as they flew, the air around me shook and pounded with the noise generated by their powerful blades.

As I heard them landing down by the power plant, I stood up and continued my walk to the barn and eventually to the shelter. I was careful to wrap my shirt around my shoulder as to keep a trail of blood from giving away our hiding place. I entered the subterranean corridor leading to the shelter and then banged on the shelter door announcing, "It's me, let me in."

The door was opened for me by Jim. I walked into the shelter while still holding my shirt wrapped around my shoulder and sat down on the first available bench space I saw.

Dan's wife Susan, who had been a nurse in the Marine Corps, began tending to my shoulder using the shelter first aid kit.

"The bullet went straight though, which is good. But upon exiting through your shoulder blade it took a chunk the size of a half-dollar with it. We'll bandage you up and hope for the best."

"Here's the first-aid kit," exclaimed Dan as he set the metal box on its back for Susan to open.

As she cleaned, disinfected, and dressed the wound, John was busy on the shortwave radio sending Morse code signals to area military troops explaining the events we witnessed at the nuclear power plant. After the wound was fully bandaged by Susan, and my left arm was wrapped in a sling, I sat onto the floor, rested the right side of my head on the wooden bench, and fell into a stupor.

"Only in death can an honest man find peace and tranquility from his transgressors."

A note scribbled into Andrew Henry's diary
February 22, 2004, at approximately 3 A.M.

Chapter Twelve: A Somber Moment

I must have fallen asleep since I appeared to awake to a nocturnal setting. All in our shelter were sleeping save me, and the shelter was dark except for the faint glow of a kerosene lamp near the commode and the amber light on the short-wave radio that glowed from the battery positioned beneath John's card table.

Strongly aware that any movement would generate tremendous pain in my wounded shoulder, I remained in my seated position on the floor with my head still resting on the shelter bench. With my eyes open, and with somber attitude, I began to read some of the newsworthy articles and poems that, I presume, John and his father had posted on walls many years earlier. I could tell that these postings were old by the yellow tint on the paper and the yellow and brittle nature of the tape holding their respective pieces to the shelter wall. The first piece that I read was as follows:

The Charge of the Light Brigade
by Alfred Tennyson

Half a league, half a league,
Half a league onward,
All in the valley of Death
Rode the six hundred.
"Forward, the Light Brigade!
"Charge for the guns!" he said:

Into the valley of Death
Rode the six hundred.
"Forward, the Light Brigade!"
Was there a man dismay'd?
Not tho' the soldier knew
Someone had blunder'd"
Their's not to make reply,
Their's not to reason why,
Their's but to do and die:
Into the valley of Death
Rode the six hundred.

Cannon to the right of them,
Cannon to left of them,
Cannon in front of them
Volley'd and thunder'd;
Storm'd at with shot and shell,
Boldly they rode and well,
Into the jaws of Death,
Into the mouth of Hell
Rode the six hundred.

Flash'd all their sabres bare,
Flash'd as they turn'd in air,
Sabring the gunners there,
Charging an army, while
All the world wonder'd:
Plunged in the battery-smoke
Right thro' the line they broke;
Cossack and Russian
Reel'd from the sabre stroke
Shatter'd and sunder'd.
Then they rode back, but not
Not the six hundred.

Cannon to the right of them,
Cannon to left of them,
Cannon behind them
Volley'd and thunder'd;
Storm'd at with shot and shell,
While horse and hero fell,
They that had fought so well
Came thro' the jaws of Death
Back from the mouth of Hell,
All that was left of them,
Left of six hundred.

When can their glory fade?
O the wild charge they made!
All the world wondered.
Honour the charge they made,
Honour the Light Brigade,
Noble six hundred.

—

After reading Tennyson's poem, and being moved by its meaning, my eyes scanned the wall before me, slightly further, until they fell to a large sheet of paper containing the following statistics:

A History of American War Deaths

(Based on the current geographic area of the United States).

War Name	American Participants	American Deaths in Service	Total Population at Time of Conflict.	Deaths as a % of the Total Pop. at Time of Conflict.
American Indians (All Tribes combined) defending America from invading forces. 1590 – 1876	An unknown number of native American Indians	An unknown number of native American Indians	An unknown number of native American Indians from all American tribes.	The highest rate of any war involving Americans.
American Revolution 1775-1784	290,000*	4,000*	3,800,000**	.11%
War of 1812 1812-1815	287,000*	2,000*	7,800,000**	.03%
Mexican War 1846-1848	79,000*	13,000*	19,700,000**	.07%
Civil War 1861-1865	3,213,000*	497,821*	35,200,000**	1.41%

Spanish-American War 1898-1902	392,000*	11,000*	75,600,000**	.02%
World War I 1917-1918	4,744,000*	116,000*	101,900,000**	.11%
World War II 1940-1947	16,535,000*	406,000*	136,200,000**	.30%
Korean Conflict 1950-1955	6,807,000*	55,000*	150,100,000**	.04%
Vietnam Era 1961-1975	9,200,000*	109,000*	194,700,000**	.06%`
Persian Gulf War 1990 statistics only	3,531,000*	5,729*	249,440,000**	.002%

* *These statistics are attributed to the National Veteran's Affaires and Rehabilitation Commission bulletin dated April 17, 1997.*

** *These statistics were obtained from the U.S. Census Bureau documents provided in ten-year increments. My numbers are based on a time-weighted average for the period.*

Note: Except for row one, the statistics typically do not include the Native American Indian population.

It struck me as interesting that America had been conquered by an enemy force once before, and the descendants of that war were still in concentration camps that we, the conquerors, more favorably call Indian reservations. It also was interesting to see that we, conquerors of American land, have been at war for more years in our history than we have been at peace (336 yrs. vs. 78 yrs. appx.). The point that this revelation drove home, is this: Since war has always been a significant part of human nature, why do the liberals typically insist that we reduce the size of our military defense capabilities?

The next article I read from its place on our shelter wall was a clipping from an old newspaper article. It read as follows: *"We're in greater danger today than we were the day after Pearl Harbor. Our Military is absolutely incapable of defending this country." --Ronald Reagan.* This article had been cut from the New York Times newspaper dated April 12, 1980.

"How ya' doin' Andrew," John asked, as he unintentionally interrupted my concentration regarding the effects these articles were having on my intellect.

"Fine, but my shoulder's killing me."

"Susan and I have called in a doctor from a neighboring militia cell. They're going to come under the cover of darkness, and hope to sneak in here by sunrise."

"What time is it?" I asked John, without wanting to move my head or left arm to view my own watch.

"3:00 A.M."

"Thanks for not using that darn military-time gibberish."

John chuckled at my humor as he saw me painfully stretch my legs out farther onto the shelter floor and lean my back against the bench in an awkward sitting position.

"John?"

"Yea."

"Now that the kids are asleep can I ask you a bunch of questions?"

"Shoot!"

We both looked at each other with astonishment at his thoughtless remark and began laughing. The harder we tried to hold back the noise from our laughter, the more my shoulder hurt and the more my laughs turned into a series of grunts and groans that seemed all the more comical. The more I tried to stop laughing and grunting, the worse it got until John's wife Sharon yelled at us to 'keep it down' and we were finally able to get our ridiculous demeanors back in check.

As we sat there in the dimly lit room attempting to regain our composure, we continued to chuckle to ourselves intermittently for about a five-minute period. I then began asking John a series of questions.

"If those dopes blow up the nuclear power plant, there would be a radiation plume, correct?"

"Yep. But I don't think they would, unless provoked. It appears that they want our power plants as sources for plutonium."

"If they did blow it up, like they did to a few nuclear power plants in the Northeast, how would you keep the radiation from seeping into this shelter?"

"When my family installed this concrete fallout shelter in the early 1960's, we designed it to protect us from nuclear radiation. We put lead inside the concrete floor, walls, and ceiling. The total wall thickness of our shelter is only slightly less than two full meters, and there is dirt all around this thing for further protection."

"What would keep the radiation from coming through your air duct?"

"We bring our air in through a vent in the floor. From the floor vent, the air intake pipe meanders up to an area one-third of a meter beneath the earth's surface. By the time the air is filtered through the earth above the ventilation intake spout, and then through our own HEPA filtration system, it should be clear enough of radiation that we wouldn't become deathly ill. It may not be foolproof, but it's better than standing out in the open and breathing unfiltered air. In addition, we zigzagged the ventilation pipe under the ground. Radiation tends to travel in a straight line, and we thought that the zigzag pipe pattern would also detour particles from entering via our air vent. Our exhaust vent pushes the air out in a similar manner, thus eliminating the seepage of any radioactivity into the shelter via our ventilation exhaust line."

"How does the air know which route to take, exit or intake?"

"We have diaphragms set up on both the intake and exhaust lines so that air can only come in on the intake line and it can only push out through the exhaust line."

"What is the HEPA filter that you mentioned?"

"HEPA is the acronym for High Efficiency Particulate Air filter. We purchased those filters years ago, and we replace them regularly so that they don't become brittle or clogged and ineffective."

"Where does the commode discharge go?"

"When we flush the john it follows a pipe out under the barn floor and empties fifty-feet away into a leach field that runs away from our shelter. In that way, the spring water under this shelter or the spring water for the house, will not become contaminated."

"Couldn't the radiation enter the ground in the leach field area and follow the pipe into our shelter?"

"I don't think so since there is water in the trap and the bowl of the john at all times, but who knows for sure? We built this thing the best we could, but it might not be foolproof. We just want to minimize our exposure so that we don't become deathly ill from the intense outside exposure that's guaranteed. You bring up an interesting point however. With all the information on today's Internet, try to find out how to build a nuclear fall-out shelter. That type of information is simply not available. Our design was based on the Civil Defense data provided back in the 1950's. Since the chance for a nuclear disaster or nuclear attack is greater today then it was in the 50's, you would think that there would be plenty of information and schematics available, but there are not."

"How long will we need to stay in here?"

"Until those guys down the hill get out of here or until our military forces them out," answered John.

"If they did blow up the power plant and a plume of radiation was emitted, how long would we need to stay in here?"

"Long enough for the main plume to blow over and then we would have to leave the area forever. When the Chernobyl power plant in the Ukraine exploded, 135,000 people had to be evacuated from a thirty-kilometer mile radius of the plant. They still have not been allowed to return. This shelter will provide protection until the major plume of radioactive particles blow over, but soon after, we would have to leave this farm forever, leaving our contaminated belongings behind."

"What would you do about the cows and horse?"

"Open the gates and let them fend for themselves," was John's reply. "I suppose that if I found any of them suffering from immediate radiation burns I would put them our of their misery before we left the area, but I wouldn't take a lot of time doing so in order to minimize my own exposure."

"Why did the enemy invade San Francisco? It's not a military or political metropolis like D.C. or New York."

"We found out that they invaded San Francisco Bay and are now dug into our shores using the bay as a base of operations to fight from. The bay offers their ships a port of protection from both our naval force and ocean storms. Our naval group from Pearl Harbor is now a few nautical miles of the coast of California sending missiles into our own coastal land areas in their attempt to regain control of the region. To someone flying overhead, it would appear that we are the enemy attacking our shores instead of them."

"John, I'm tired now so I want to get some rest."

"O.K., I'll leave you alone. Are you comfortable? Can I get you a blanket or something?"

"I wouldn't mind some aspirin and a glass of water for my shoulder pain."

"Comin' right up."

As John opened the first aid kit for aspirin and then went to the sink for a glass of water, I pulled his three-year-old son Michael to my chest and rocked him while he slept. "You don't mind if I hold Michael, do you?" I asked John when he returned with my aspirin and water.

"Na'," was his reply. "I'm sure Michael will love the attention although he sleeps like a log so I doubt he'll even realize that your holding him."

"Thanks," I said, as I grabbed the aspirin with my right hand and inserted them into my mouth. I then grabbed the water glass from John, swallowed, and set the glass beside me on the floor. As he went back to bed, I rocked little Michael and reminisced about my daughter Kelly when she was this age. I longed for the sweet smell of my baby, --that pleasant fragrance that emanated from her forehead and her hair when she was in a deep sleep in my arms. I longed to hold her living body to me again, and protect her and rock her to sleep, as I was rocking and protecting Michael. I longed to . . .

With the arrival of morning, I was abruptly awakened to the sobbing noises of John's wife blended with the hysterical crying noises of her two children.

"She's dead," responded Susan while looking directly at me. "Mrs. Cindrich passed away in the night," she told me, as I woke and looked around in a slightly dazed state from the commotion. "The severe strain of this ordeal must have been too much for her frail eighty-five year old frame," she concluded before standing and moving over to the sink area.

With the hecticness caused by Mrs. Cindrich's death besieging the shelter, I instinctively started to stand but was immediately pulled back to my seating position by the pain in my shoulder.

"Ugh," I groaned, as I grabbed my left shoulder with my right arm. "Oh boy, I'm in trouble," I added, as I noticed that my entire shoulder area had swollen and become extremely painful.

Susan came to my aid, carrying a glass of water, and peeked into my bandages.

"It's infected isn't it?"

"I'm afraid it's going to be," responded Susan, "and we don't have any antibiotics down here. If the doctor doesn't show up soon, someone will have to drive you to a hospital inland somewhere."

As the adults of our group carried Mrs. Cindrich out to the hill overlooking the Ohio River for burial, I remained behind to nurse my shoulder. The two children followed the procession, crying and carrying on dreadfully all the way out.

After everyone left, I painfully rose to use the commode. I relished this opportunity of privacy, since there were no walls protecting the commode or shower area from visual scrutiny. After use, I walked to the kitchen sink and painfully washed my face and removed the bandages from my shoulder. I gingerly washed the front of the wound and then placed a fresh gauze pad to both sides of my shoulder. I rewrapped new bandages around the gauze pads, since the old wraps were completely drenched with my blood. After this painful process, I once again became exhausted and faint. I returned to my sitting position on the shelter floor and again rested my head on the bench behind me.

About an hour-and-a-half later, all returned to the protection of our shelter and the last to enter shut the door behind him.

"How long do we have to remain here?" questioned John's wife, Sharon, with the two children standing somberly behind her.

"Until the regular military arrives so that we can help them in their counterattack against the enemy soldiers stationed at the power plant," said John.

"Why don't we just give up and drive away?" suggested Susan. "Andrew's shoulder is becoming infected, and this is no place for the children. Besides, if the power plant is destroyed during our attack, either by our attacking forces, or as a part of a 'scorch and burn' campaign by the enemy, we'll be stuck down here for at least a week to avoid the adverse effects of the initial radiation plume."

"You're right, Susan," said John. "Let's eat breakfast right now, in the shelter, and we'll then depart."

"I hate to leave the farm and the animals alone and undefended," mentioned Sharon, "but there's nothing more we can do here," she said to John.

He nodded in agreement as he pulled a can of hash from the kitchen cabinet above the stove and began opening it with a hand-held can opener.

"They turned off the power last night," said John, "so we can't use the electric hot plate. But we can at least eat a hearty, cold, canned-good breakfast before we go."

"Anyone want peaches?" Jim asked as he passed the can to Debbie who had raised her hand first.

As we all sat there eating our individual breakfast selections from a can, I began to ask more questions.

"John?"

"Yea, Andrew."

"What if we launched one last attack against those bastards at the power plant before we go? I would love to inflict revenge for the deaths of my wife and daughter and I am certain that you feel the same regarding the death of your mom."

"Well they probably share the same passion for revenge that you're exhibiting and that I feel at this very moment. You need to remember that many of the countries that are now invading us possess a hatred against Americans that stems back many generations. With passions running that deep, they won't be discouraged easily and we're outnumbered, especially with your injured shoulder."

"In addition to passion," added Dan, "it takes technology to win battles and we're out gunned."

"How the heck did the enemy know where my wife and daughter were hiding in Clawson, N.Y.? You told me that each militia cell kept its identity confidential from even other member cells. Only neighboring cells and top ranking militia leaders know the whereabouts of other cells, and these guys must have had a map showing cell and shelter locations since Dan told me that my wife's shelter was not the only one discovered and raided."

"The FBI has been tracking the militia movement ever since the Oklahoma City bombing in 1994," said Jim. "They have compiled lists of every militia cell in the country since they view the U.S. Militia as a 'threat to the security of the United States'."

"What threat? We're on the same side, or at least we should be. The Oklahoma bombing wasn't done by any militia group; it was done by a couple of individuals. It was the media that wanted to give it the "U.S. Militia" spin in an attempt to sensationalize the story and generate maximum commercial impact.

"It may **not** have been the media that gave it that spin," responded Jim. "It was probably the U.S. government propaganda that started that rumor."

"The government is disgusted with militia members throughout the country, insisting that we maintain the original precepts of the constitution," said Sharon. "The government's inherent need for growth, and our virulent stand against its growth, put us at odds; therefore we are their enemy in a figurative way."

"And they will squelch any and all dissent, using any means possible," added Dan. "And in regards to the U.S. Militia, propaganda is their weapon of choice."

"The militia DOES represent a threat to the security of the United States," responded Jim, and as all eyes turned to him he continued. "The militia will not accept the social changes that must be enacted for this country to move forward. The U.S. has changed its course from the original Constitution by passing our many Constitutional Amendments and it wants to change even more. But, it has the militia to worry about since that group wants to strictly adhere to its original premise of 'the rights of the individual' that we used to enjoy. Those rights are over. Our greedy, corrupt, and gluttonous government has become so large that it now must intrude on our inalienable rights in order to perpetuate itself further. The militia is one of many groups that stand in the government's way and that is why it has been under surveillance by the FBI."

"You're implying," stated John, "that every militia cell has an FBI infiltrator directly or indirectly connected to it."

"Yes," replied Jim, "and I'm embarrassed and sorry to admit, that each regional FBI office, and field office, has a list of every shelter location in their area. So like Andrew's family, WE ARE IN DANGER HERE. All the enemy needs is that list, and. . ...."

He paused in speech and became even more uneasy as we unconsciously revealed our expressions of disgust and anguish over the realization that we had a betrayer in our midst. Jim recoiled into the corner and sat onto the bench holding his head in his hands.

"He's an undercover FBI agent," Sharon said in astonishment.

"You idiot," responded John. For the past five years you've worked in our warehouse, you were spying on us because I was a member of a militia group?"

"I'm sorry," he said. "I'm sor . . .

Interrupting Jim's last attempt at a totally unacceptable apology for his betrayal of our group, the door flew open, and the noise from gun bullets riveting the room overwhelmed my senses. As I looked about me, everyone in the room had been shot. I looked at John. His bulletproof vest had not saved him this time. Besides the blood heavily oozing from bullet holes in his vest, there were two bullet holes in his head that created a gruesome and distorted expression on his face.

It appeared that everyone in the room was slumped over and dead or unconsciously twitching in the jaws of death, save me and the girl child that had been eating peaches at my side. As she was seated on the floor between the gunman, and me, she immediately recoiled into my lap, crying and burrowing her face into my flannel shirt, the best she could, for protection. Realizing that I was fatally wounded, with bullet wounds to my right leg and abdomen adding to the pain of my left shoulder, I scanned the room for assistance but saw none available. Everyone had now ceased twitching; including Jim, our-well intentioned but severely misled FBI informant. Beneath the bench, where he was sitting, was a puddle of urine from his now uncontrolled bladder.

I turned my head to look up at our assailant. His gun barrel was pointed at my head, from the door entrance where he stood motionless. Behind him I could see at least two additional men standing with their guns drawn as well. As I looked back to the soldier in the doorway, I could see that he was wearing khaki/green clothing with a red-colored beret cap. The cap was similar to the ones worn by the New York City-based Guardian Angels back in the 1990's. There was a metal insignia in the front, but I could not discern its meaning or national origin. His pants had several bulging pockets on the sides, and his black, shin-high military boots were covered with mud. Tied around his ankle, just above his right boot, was a five-inch knife encased in a sheath. As I wearily looked up past the small opening in his gun barrel, I peered into his eyes with mine. As his eyelids and brow began to squint, his eyes became more and more recessed. I could see in them a reflection of the look that I knew I used to possess, in my youth, as both a hunter of wild game and as a slayer of foot-trapped furbearers. The man's demeanor was now set in the mode of heartless killer, and his resolve was cast. Then, I could see his eyes squint further, a flash from the barrel of his gun, and. . .

The ability of Andrew Henry to enter this final diary notation will be explained in the next chapter.

- The End-

Epilogue

Twenty Years Later, December 2, 2024:

As a part of my thesis paper in historical studies at Wellsville College, Ohio, I have written this story based on Andrew Henry's diary. Area rescue workers had discovered the fallout shelter and bodies a full two months after the second wave of the invasion had been thwarted by a united American front. Andrew's diary was found behind his severely decayed corpse as it laid under the bench that he had been leaning against when he was shot. It is suspected that Andrew regained consciousness for a short time after the shooting, since he had been able to enter the final description of his assailant into his diary before death. --There was blood all over that diary's final page, adding further credence to our theory.

The little six-year-old girl's remains were found coiled in her deceased mother's lap. It is not known whether the same assailant had killed her or whether she had starved to death since, in later interviews, rescue workers reported finding no bullet holes in her remains. She and the others were buried without an autopsy being conducted, which was common practice in those days immediately following the war. We shall never know for certain how the girl died, but we can hope and pray that she had not been locked inside alive, to suffer a hideous and lonely death.

Less than four weeks after the death of Andrew Henry, his family, and his friends, the war turned in our favor. The U.S. Military, along with the U.S. Militia, and millions upon millions of American citizens bearing small arms, were a combined force great enough to push the invading troops back out of our country. Now, since that war fought twenty years ago, much has changed in America.

Like the post-World War II Japanese cities of Nagasaki and Hiroshima, the war-ravaged cities of Washington and San Francisco have been re-built. What was once New York City is now a landfill area like its neighbor, Staten Island. Thousands of U.S. citizens on each coast have died from various forms of cancer attributed to the radiation exposure they received during and after the war, --but there is hope that springs from every war.

It is a hope that we will become stronger, more united, and better prepared against any foreign enemy for the benefit of future generations of Americans. It is the realization that even in our diversity, Americans still cherish the same basic principals of freedom and independence from any tyrannous regime. And it is a resolve that history shall not repeat itself as long as those who know it well, remember its lessons.

Although our spending on defense has been increased since the war (for obvious reasons), the overall government has been reduced twenty percent in size, thereby proportionally reducing our collective tax rate from 59.1 percent to a more affordable 39.1 percent of our gross annual income. The American people now have money to spend realizing their own dreams, as opposed to working solely to satisfy the dreams of an unwieldy and oppressive government.

We must be cautious, however, as we look to the future. In this year of 2024, better health care has increased the average American citizen's life expectancy to 89 years of age for women and 83 years for men. This trend has led to an increase in apartment living. When Andrew Henry was alive, twenty years ago, only five percent of our population lived in apartments. That rate has now increased to twenty-five percent of the population. The concern is that our current tax laws still fail to tax apartment renters for our public school programs. As a result, renters are voting for school program/tax increases in alarming numbers to the dismay of property owners who must fund the bills. I feel that those who vote for any tax increases must share in their burden or not participate in the vote. Failure to enact this common sense, and fair, requirement would risk collective tax rates escalating back to the oppressive 59.1 percent rate of 1999 for those hard-working men and women who are required to pay them. --This is discrimination and discrimination, in any form, should be illegal in America.

Another concern is that the number of retired citizens has increased from being fifteen percent to thirty-one percent of the American voting force. Now that the full spectrum of baby-boomers have retired, retirees are filling the voting booths in record numbers for every issue. The concern is that retiree's pay no New York State income tax on their social security checks or pension checks. Realizing this, government unions are encouraging retirees to vote "YES" for State programs which will increase the working man's State income tax, but not that of the retiree voter. Again, if a citizen will not be funding a program through increased taxes to his person, he/she should not be allowed to vote. The funding of government programs must be shared by all who vote for them or an imbalance will exist, which will cause dissention, strife, and discrimination.

Disclaimer

This book is a work of fiction. Names, characters, places, and incidents are the products of the author's imagination or are used fictitiously.

- ADDENDUM I –

AMERICAN TAX FACTS AND AUTHOR'S LECTURE: THE RICH DO PAY THEIR FAIR SHARE IN TAXES.

To anyone espousing the rhetorical and fallacious argument that; *'...the rich don't pay their fair share of taxes,'* I have a strong and poignant a message: You are a liar and an intentional deceiver since United States tax laws are based on an ascending scale that definitively requires the rich pay a far higher tax rate than the poor in every tax category. –How much of a financial penalty can one impose against the best producers in our society before they become discouraged and counterproductive? --Just because they work harder and smarter than you do, does not mean that you are entitled to their earnings. And if you are simply jealous because an individual was born into wealth, then shame on you for thinking that you can use the government as a tool to rob them of their inheritance. Your monetary lust and jealous vises will never be squelched, no mater how much we tax the rich, penalize the rich, or discriminate against the rich. If you more honestly stated that you wanted, *'...the rich to pay more in taxes than they already do, simply because I am envious of them,'* then I would better appreciate your candid argument. But, there is a very serious problem with that position as well. As we heighten our discriminatory tax practices against the rich, we cross (in equal increments) from a socialistic society to a communistic regime, and history has dramatically proven that system to be unfair and counterproductive to everyone but the politicians who thrive in that tightly regulated and governmentally corrupt environment. Communism is economically and socially crippling to any nation that implements its mechanisms of coercive taxation and excessive regulation. **But in**

addressing my original point, following is proof that the 'rich' do pay more than their fair share in taxes:

EXAMPLE REFERENCING 2001 INCOME TAX STATUES:

I. **Federal Payroll Net Income Tax Form #1040:**

Welfare joint income earners pay .... 0 %
in Federal Income Taxes.
(But they can vote for tax increases on the rest of us.)
100% Disabled joint income earners pay....... 0%
in Federal Income Taxes.
(But they can vote for tax increases on the rest of us.)
$0 - $27,050 joint income earners pay....**15%**
in Federal Income Taxes.
$27,051 - 65,550 joint income earners pay....27.5% in Federal Income Taxes.
$65,551 - $136,750 joint income earners pay 30.5% in Federal Income Taxes.
$136,751-$297,350 joint income earners pay 35.5% in Federal Income Taxes.
$297,351 –and up joint income earners **pay 39.1%**
in Federal Income Taxes.
(Note: However you compute the math, the rich are negatively discriminated against and they do pay much more in taxes than the poor.)

II. **New York State Net Income Tax Rates:**

Welfare joint income earners pay..................0%
in State Income Taxes.
(But they can vote for tax increases on the rest of us.)
Federal and State retired workers
(age 55 and up) pay..................................0%
in State Income Taxes.
(But they can vote for tax increases on the rest of us.)
$0 - $16,000 join income earners pay......4%

in State Income Taxes.
$16,001 – $22,000 joint income earners pay.....4.5% in State Income Taxes.
$22,001 - $26,000 joint income earners pay..... 5.25% in State Income Taxes.
$26,001 - $40,000 joint income earners pay......5.9% in State Income Taxes.
$40,001 – and up joint income earners pay .... 8.5% in State Income Taxes.
(Note: However you do the math, the rich are negatively discriminated against and they do pay much more in taxes than the poor.)

III. Property Tax Rates (School, County, Town, Village, Sewer, Water, & Fire Combined Taxes):
Poor people (if apartment dwellers): ....0% NYS Property Taxes.
I.e. If a home has three family apartments the property tax amount that the landlord pays is the same as if it was a 1 family home. As a result, two Tenants effectively pay 0% in NYS property taxes. *(But they can vote on school tax increases that the rest of us must pay for.)*
Medium income people (homeowner):..........2.6%-7% " "
Rich people (homeowner): .... Significantly more in dollars.*
*(Note: *1. The more affluent the community, the more the property owner pays in taxes. The poorer the community, generally, the lower the tax rate.*

2. *However you compute the math, the rich are negatively discriminated against and they do pay much more in taxes than the poor. More importantly, the rich may not receive any more in service benefits than the poor in their community, even though they are required to pay far more in taxes. –This is not fair, this*

is despicably discriminatory. I believe that all should pay for our school systems, not just property owners. A school tax based upon a percentage of one's income, versus property ownership, would be a fairer system. –Let everyone contribute, not just property owners, and the burden then becomes more equitably shared.

3. *New York State residents pay school taxes via a property tax because legislators believe in the unsubstantiated notion that homeowners are more affluent than apartment dwellers. As a result, apartment dwellers (many of whom are wealthy) are not required to pay school taxes in New York State. Some other states use a more equitable and less discriminatory tax based on net personal income as opposed to property tax to generate their school and service revenues.)*

IV. Capitol Gains Tax:

The rich pay a Federal capital gains tax of 15% on the first $50,000 in gains and higher graduated rates up from there. This is a tax on investment gains before the rich even get a chance to cash their investments in and reward themselves with any extra income. When they sell their investment and take the gain as income, it is taxed as ordinary income via the New York State statutes (8.5%), but the Federal rate varies from 20% up to your highest ordinary tax bracket percentage (30.5% - 39.1%). *(Note: However you do the math, the rich are negatively discriminated against and they do pay much more in taxes than the poor.)*

V. Interest/Dividend Tax:

This is a marginal rate added to regular income. Therefore, as shown in the above Federal and State payroll income tax tables the rich pay a higher tax rate for this income, than the poor, as well. *(Note: However you do the math, the rich are negatively discriminated against and they do pay much more in taxes than the poor.)*

VI. State Inheritance Tax/Estate Tax (double taxation):

Tax rate for an estate worth $0-$710,000..................0% estate tax rate.
Tax rate for an estate worth $710,000 or more............3% estate tax rate.
(Note: However you do the math, the rich are negatively discriminated against and they do pay much more in taxes than the poor.)

VII. Federal Inheritance Tax/Estate Tax (double taxation):

Tax rate for an estate worth $0-710,000....................0% Fed. estate tax
Tax rate for an estate worth $710,000 or more: 10%-50%.
(Note: However you do the math, the rich are negatively discriminated against and they do pay much more in taxes than the poor.)

VIII. Corporate Tax (New York State):

The rich pay an 8% Corporate Tax on all net profit generated by their company, even if this profit is saved for future investments, emergencies, or pending law suits. This means that the corporation owner pays a tax for earnings that he doesn't even get to personally spend.
(Note: However you compute the math, the rich are negatively discriminated against and they do pay much more in taxes than the poor.)

IX. Corporate Inventory Tax (New York State): Variable by company.

X. Social Security Income Tax Rate:...............
(State)..........(Federal).
$0-$10,000 in joint family income......... 0%
0% State Tax and 0% Federal Tax
More than $10,000...............................up to 85% of the SS income based on the amt. of additional income earned by the couple.
(Note: However you compute the math, the rich are negatively discriminated against and they do pay much more in taxes than the poor.)

XI. Medicare Income Tax Rate:
0-100,000 in joint family income...........................1.5%
More than $100,000 in joint family income................2.5%
(Note: However you compute the math, the rich are negatively discriminated against and they do pay much more in taxes than the poor.)

SUMMARY –

As shown in the prior examples, using the argument that the rich don't pay their fair share in taxes is fallacious and malicious, but I fully understand the three reasons for these phenomena.

Reason I: Politicians like Massachusetts Senator Ted Kennedy and New York State Senator Hillary Clinton use this diatribe to secure votes from the poor, the lazy, the unlucky, the socialists, the communists, and the seemingly disenfranchised in our society. It is this unsubstantiated rhetoric, coupled with a news media that perpetuates this myth, that keeps politicians like these in office and in power. But to these wealthy politicians, I would propose the following concept: "Only when a man/woman has as little as I do, should he/she ask me to give more." *(James, Andrew, "The Song, The Best Poets of 2001, International Library of Poetry", Watermark Press, Owings Mills, MD., ©1999, p. 50.)*

Reason II: Some people, but very few, are truly kind and generous. They themselves have sacrificed most of their worldly possessions to help others in their community and/or throughout the world. These martyrs have a just right to propose the exaggerated claim that the rich, 'don't pay their fair share in taxes'. Although their montra is not actually factual, they have earned the right to employ overstated arguments, like this, due to their own commitment of self sacrifice and example. In their view, no one should have more than his/her neighbor and the weak should be protected by the strong. –True martyrs are seldom vocal, but when they are, they possess a hard earned right to express their views from their perspective. --At least this group is not as hypocritical as the many wealthy politicians, pseudo religious leaders, or movie stars who implement this argument devoid of significant personal example. "For only when you are as poor as I, should you ask me to give more" *(James 50).*

Reason III: Most people who use the argument that, 'the rich don't pay their fair share of taxes', are simply jealous of the success of others.They feel disenfranchised and out of the loop of affluence, but are unwilling or unable to earn their way in. They feel cheated somehow and, as a result, they desire to take from the rich the property, the prosperity, and /or the income that they feel should be theirs. In this example, the need to excessively tax the rich stems more from a philosophy of revenge than one of avarice.

Now, for those die-hards who still don't believe that the rich pay their fair share of taxes, I propose another more specific example:

Specific Example:
I... Bill Gates III, Chairman & CEO of Microsoft Corp.
Personal Ranking: One of the world's richest individuals,

(Forbes Magazine, 1999).*

Corporate Ranking: 5th largest U.S. Corporation (Fortune Magazine, 1999).

No. U.S. Employees: 5.2 Million (Fortune Magazine, 1999)**

Corporate 1999 Income before income taxes: $11.8 Billion Dollars***

Corporate 1999 Income taxes paid: $ 4.1 Billion Dollars***
(35% Corporate Tax)***.

Corporate 1999 inventory taxes paid: $1.2 Billion Dollars est.

*(Less: 1999 Local and State Corporate Tax rebates Received:**** ($ 53.2 Million Dollars) est.*

TOTAL NET CORPORATE TAXES PAID: 4.8 Billion Dollars***

(41% of Corp. Revenue)

Plus:
Bill Gates' 1999 personal income:*****
$542,297 Dollars
Bill Gates' 1999 personal state income taxes paid:
43,384 (8%)
Bill Gates' 1999 personal Federal income taxes paid:
212,038 (39.1%)
Bill Gates' 1999 personal Social Security taxes paid:
34,165 (6.3%)
Bill Gates' 1999 personal Medicare taxes paid:
8,135 (1.5%)
Bill Gates' 1999 total U.S. personal property taxes paid:
68,000 (1.3%)
Bill Gates' 1999 total personal sewer taxes paid:
1,200
Bill Gates' 1999 total personal water taxes paid:
1,200
Bill Gates' 1999 personal license fees paid:
995

Bill Gates' 1999 hidden taxes & surcharges for U.S. hotels and motel surcharge taxes, telephone surcharge taxes, auto fuel surcharge taxes, home heating fuel surcharge taxes, electric surcharge taxes, liquor surcharge taxes, luxury items surcharge taxes, etc:.........................51,520 (10%)
Bill Gates' 1999 family health expense surcharge tax as charged by all emergency rooms and doctors' offices:........... 5,200 est. (.1%)
Bill Gates' personal spending state and local sales taxes paid on personal product purchases:
8,135 est.
Bill Gates' total estimated 1999 personal taxes paid: $433,972 (80%)
Plus: Capital gains tax on personal stockholding liquidations: 271,149 est.
Plus: Corporate income taxes paid in 1999:
4.8 Billion***
TOTAL TAXES PAID BY BILL GATES PERSONALLY AND VIA MICROSOFT CORPORATE TAXES: .... Over $4.8 Billion

THANK GOD THAT THE RICH ARE CONTRIBUTING MORE THAN THEIR FAIR SHARE OF TAX DOLLARS, OR THE REST OF US WOULD NEED TO PAY MORE!
*(Source: *Forbes Magazine, New York: 1999.*
***Fortune Magazine, Fortune 500 Companies, New York: p. 37 1999.*
****Microsoft 1999 Annual Report/Corporate Income Statement. 1999.*
*****Estimated total collective U.S. local, state, and Federal tax break rebates.*
******www.boardoptions.com/ychightechsalary.htm*
Stybel, Peabody, & Associates, Inc. "Trends in High Tech Compensation:
Salary Survey-Executive Compensation." Stybel, Peabody, & Assoc., Inc.
1999.

Note: Please apply the previous tax rate formula matrix to any corporation or wealthy individual before making the naïve and baseless assumption that the rich don't pay their fair share in taxes. –They pay more than their fair share!

Corporate annual reports are available on the internet and they include a section showing the amount each corporation pays in taxes. The total corporate taxes paid, less community/state refunds received, plus community/ state donations, reflects the total net taxes paid by that corporation. (And the amounts are significant).

Further:

Americans in the top five percent of incomes pay more of the state and Federal income tax burden than any other group. **According to 1999 IRS statistics, the 6.3 million TAXPAYERS WHOSE INCOMES WERE IN THE TOP FIVE PERCENT COLLECTIVELY PAID MORE THAN FIFTY-FIVE PERCENT OF ALL U.S. INCOME TAXES.** This group had adjusted gross incomes over $120,846 a year. This means that a primary income earner and his/her spouse could earn slightly over $60,000 each, and be considered 'rich' by the Federal government.

TAXPAYERS IN THE BOTTOM HALF OF THE INCOME SPECTRUM COLLECTIVELY PAID ONLY FOUR PERCENT OF ALL U.S. INCOME TAXES in 1999. *(1999 IRS Statistics)*. So the rich do pay MORE THAN their fair share in taxes, and to say otherwise is not only fallacious, but also malicious, moronic, and irresponsible. One must state that they simply want to, 'tax the rich more,' in order to be accurate, not that; 'the rich don't pay their fair share,' because **statistically the 'rich' do pay more than their fair share in taxes**.

–APPENDIX A–

THE RICH DO PAY MORE THAN THEIR FAIR SHARE IN TAXES: FEDERAL TAX RATE TABLE.

-- APPENDIX A --

The rich do pay more than their fair share in taxes.

2001 Tax Rate Schedules - Line 16 (Source: Federal Income Tax Form #1040 preparation instruction booklet)

Schedule X—Use if your **2001** filing status was **Single**

If Schedule J, line 15, is: *Over—*	*But not over—*	Enter on Schedule J, line 16	*of the amount over—*
$0	$27,050	.... 15%	$0
27,050	65,550	$4,057.50 + 27.5%	27,050
65,550	136,750	14,645.00 + 30.5%	65,550
136,750	297,350	36,361.00 + 35.5%	136,750
297,350	....	93,374.00 + 39.1%	297,350

Schedule Y-2—Use if your **2001** filing status was **Married filing separately**

If Schedule J, line 15, is: *Over—*	*But not over—*	Enter on Schedule J, line 16	*of the amount over—*
$0	$22,600	...... 15%	$0
22,600	54,625	$3,390.00 + 27.5%	22,600
54,625	83,250	12,196.88 + 30.5%	54,625
83,250	148,675	20,927.50 + 35.5%	83,250
148,675	....	44,153.38 + 39.1%	148,675

Schedule Y-1—Use if your **2001** filing status was **Married filing jointly** or **Qualifying widow(er)**

If Schedule J, line 15, is: *Over—*	*But not over—*	Enter on Schedule J, line 16	*of the amount over—*
$0	$45,200	.... 15%	$0
45,200	109,250	$6,780.00 + 27.5%	45,200
109,250	166,500	24,393.75 + 30.5%	109,250
166,500	297,350	41,855.00 + 35.5%	166,500
297,350	....	88,306.75 + 39.1%	297,350

Schedule Z—Use if your **2001** filing status was **Head of household**

If Schedule J, line 15, is: *Over—*	*But not over—*	Enter on Schedule J, line 16	*of the amount over—*
$0	$36,250	...... 15%	$0
36,250	93,650	$5,437.50 + 27.5%	36,250
93,650	151,650	21,222.50 + 30.5%	93,650
151,650	297,350	38,912.50 + 35.5%	151,650
297,350	......	90,636.00 + 39.1%	297,350

Note: Welfare recipients pay no federal income tax nor do social security recipients.

- APPENDIX B –

AN EXERPT FROM THE NEW YORK STATE TAX TABLES ALSO VERRIFIES THAT THE RICH PAY MORE THAN THEIR FAIR SHARE IN TAXES:

From the 1997 N.Y. State tax tables: Notice the ascending scales: The more you make = the higher tax rate you pay.			
Income Bracket:	Single or Married Filing Separately State Tax Tate:	Married Filing Jointly State Tax Rate:	Head of a Household State Tax Rate:
Welfare Recipient:	0%	0%	0%
Pension Recipient *(Not earning more than $10,000 on the side).*	0%	0%	0%
$15,000	4.5%	4.0%	4.1%%
$30,000	5.5%	4.5%	5%
$50,000	6.1%	5.3%	5.7%
$65,000 - $150,000	9.3%	8.5%	8.1%
More than $150,000	12.3%	11.7%	12%

Note: Welfare recipients pay <u>no</u> state income tax nor do social security recipients.

(Unless they earn supplemental income.)

- ADDENDUM II –

THE COMMUNIST MANIFESTO

The major theme for a communistic state is stated within The Communist Manifesto, as written by Karl Marx and Fredrich Engles. It was published for their 1848 League of Communist meeting in London, England (Encarta, The Communist Manifesto 1). It was thereafter distributed throughout the world in the hope that fellow communists would embrace its philosophy and united behind its instructions. The goal of the manifesto was for the citizenry of every nation to, "wrest by degrees" (Bender 74), the capital from the wealthy and redistribute it to the poor. They were to achieve this trough labor unionization and revolt. There are ten essential treaties highlighted within the manifesto. While these points seemed atrocious to most Americans in 1848, the socialist movement and its many veiled communist members have already achieved some of their original goals through the use of persistence, tenacity, and stealth. Following are the key points of The Communist Manifesto as outlined within said document:

1. "Abolition of property in land and application of all rents of land to public purposes" (Hutchings 429 & Bender 74).

2. "A heavy progressive or graduated income tax" (ibid).

3. "Abolition of all right of inheritance" (ibid).

4. "Confiscation of the property of all emigrants and rebels" (ibid).

5. "Centralization of credit in the hands of the state by means of a national bank with state capital and exclusive monopoly" (ibid).

6. "Centralization of the means of communication and transport in the hands of the state" (ibid).

7. “Extension of factories and instruments of production owned by the state; the bringing improvement of the soil generally in accordance with a common plan” (ibid).

8. “Equal obligation of all to work. Establishment of industrial armies, especially for agriculture” (ibid).

9. “Combination of agriculture with manufacturing industries; gradual abolition of the distinction between town and country by a more equable distribution of the population over the country” (ibid).

10. “Free education for all children in public schools. Abolition of child factory labour in its present form. Combination of education with industrial production, etc.” (ibid).

The above shall be done, according to Marx, in an effort to eliminate class or religious distinctions (Hutchins 429). In essence, the needs of society will overshadow the rights of the individual and all shall become equal. The individual’s potential will be defined by the government or by social dictate as opposed to work ethic, talent, religious affiliation, or ability.

- ADDENDUM III –

A LIST OF COMMUNIST ORGANIZATIONS

Following is a list of communist organizations throughout the world. The list is expansive, but not all-inclusive. We know that there are many more proud and devout communists, even within the boarders of a free America, but we do not hear the title spoken often enough. We do not see their party tout its existence, nor do we hear the term, 'communist', in numbers that aptly reflect American party subscription. What we do see and hear is the rampant ranting that, "...the rich should pay more in taxes," but via that mantra alone, they expose themselves:

- AKE Progressive Party of Working People (Cyprus)
- Alliance Marxist-Leninist (North America)
- All-Union Leninist Communist Union of Youth – Obinsk
- Anti-Capitalist Union
- Alsynechia Revolutionary Marxist Organization (Greece)
- Alternative Socialista Luta e Solidaridade
- Arbeidernes Kommunist parti
- Arbertarnas Sida (Workers' Page.Sweden)
- Belfast Socialist Party
- Bexley and Greenwich Socialist Party
- Bloomington Solidarity
- BWK Bundes Westdeutscher Kommunisten
- Cem Tiz
- Centro Internacional del Trotskismo Orthodoxo (CITO)
- Class War Union
- CiberLeninist
- Circolo Rifondazione Comunista-Pianura (Napoli)
- Colectivo de Jovenes Comunistas Alicante
- Committee for a Workers International
- Partido Comunista de los Pueblos de Espana
- Comite' para a Internacional Operaria
- Committer for a Workers International

- Communist Party of Aotearoa
- Communist Party of Australia
- Communist Party of Australia – Blacktown Branch
- Communist Party of Australia – Maritime Branch (Sydney)
- Communist Party of Brazil PcdoB
- Communist Party of Britain. Greater London East Branch
- Communist Party of Britain – Sheffield
- Communist Party of Canada
- Communist Party of Canada Ontario
- Communist Party of Canada (Marxist-Leninist)
- Communist Party of Connecticut
- Communist Party of Cyprus
- Communist Party of Behemia and
- Communist Party of Czech and Moravia
- Communist Party of Denmark/ML (DKP/ML)
- Communist Party of Greece KKE
- Communist Party of Illinois
- Communist Party of India (Marxist)
- Communist Party of India (Marxist-Leninist) People's War (CPI-ML PW)
- Communist Party of Iran
- Communist Party of Israel
- Communist Party of Luxembourg
- Communist Party of Minnesota and the Dakotas
- Communist Party of Napal (Maoist)
- Communist Party of Napal (Unified Marxist-Leninist)
- Communist Party of Peru (PCP)
- Communist Party of Sweden KPML (r)
- Communist Party of the Carolinas
- Communist Party of the District of Columbia
- Communist Party of the Philipines
- Communist Party of the Russican Federation (Kommunisticheskaya Party
- Rossiskoi Federatsii (KPRF)).
- Communist Party of the Russian Federation (KPRF) – Leningrad

- Communist Party of the Russian Federation (Youthi)
- Communist Party of the Soviet Union
- Communist Party of the Valencian Country
- Communist Party of Vietnam
- Communist Party U.S.A.
- Communist Party, KPML (r)
- Communist Refoundation Party of Italy
- Communist Workers Organization
- Communist Workers Group of New Zealand
- Communist Workers Organization
- Communist Youth League of Norway NKU
- Communist Youth of Greece KNE
- Communist Youth of Ticino (Switzerland)
- Communist Unitari
- CPS Communist Party of Slovakia
- Cyber Communist Party
- Cyber Leninism
- CyberRed
- Cyber Space Party of Socialist Students and Workers
- Democratic Socialists
- Denmarks Kommunistiske Parti Marxister-Leninister (DKP-ML)
- Deutsche Kommunistische Partei DKP
- Deutsche Kommunistische Partei Hamburg
- DHKP/L Revolutionary People's Liberation Party-Front
- DKP Deutscher Kommunistische Partei Hamburg
- DKP Deutscher Kommunistische Partei Hochschulgruppe Schleswig-Holstein
- Earlham Socialist Alliance
- En defensa del Marxismo
- EHK (Euskal Herriko Komunistak)
- European Network of the Democratic Youth Left
- Forum Unger Marxister (Forum Young Marxist. Sweden)
- Freedom Socialist Party-Revolutionary Feminist International

- Freedom Road Socialist Organization
- Freedom Road Socialist Party-Revolutionary Feminist International
- Gauche Socialiste
- Griffith University International Socialists
- Grupo Comunista Internacionalista
- Grupo Socialista Guernica
- Guelph Socialist
- Homosexuella Socialister
- Hungarian Workers Party
- ILC Workers' International Liaison Committee
- Internasjonale Socialister
- International Bolshevik Tendenaz
- International Socialist (Canada)x
- International Socialist Group (UK, not an official member)
- International Socialist Organization
- International Socialist Organization. New York City District
- International Socialist Organization.StPaul/ Minneapolis, Minnesota
- International Socialist Organization. University of Pittsburgh
- International Socialists Club
- International Socialister (in English)
- International Socialister (in Danish)
- Internationalist Communist Group
- Internationalist Communist Union (ICU)
- Iranian Communist Fadaian League
- Iranian Revolutionary Socialists League
- Irish Socialist Party
- ISKRA Communist Youth of Switzerland
- Izquierda Revolucionaria
- Japanese Communist Party JCP
- Japanese Revolutionary Communist League (Revolutionary Marxist Facti)
- Jeunesse Socialiste Revolutionnaire (JSR)
- Joventud Comunista CJC
- Joves Comunistes (Organizacion Juvenil del PSUC

viu)

- JUKO Joves Comunistes
- JUK Online Junge Kommunist Innem
- Juventud Comunista del Pais Valencia – L'Alacanti
- Juventud Socialista del MAS.Seccion Argentina de la LIT-CI
- Juventude Comunista Portuguesa
- Juventudes Comunistas de Castilla-Leon
- Kenyan Socialist
- Kommunistinuoret Communist Youth of Finland
- Kommunistisk Parti I Denmark
- Kommunistisk Parti I Denmark – Arhus
- Kommunistisk Parti I Denmark –Bornholm
- Kommunistische Partei Deutschland, Leninische/ German Communist Party, Leninist
- Kommunistiska Partiet, (revolutionarerna) KPML (r)
- Korean News
- KPO Niederosterreich
- La Red Roja de los Jovenes Comunista de la Universidad Catolica de chill
- Labor Militant Online
- Le Militant (Wallonia Belgium)
- Le Ragioni del Socialismo
- League for a Revolutionary Communist International
- League of Revolutionaries for a New America
- Leninist Young Communist League of the Soviet Union (Moscow)
- Leninist Young Communist League of the Soviet Union (Obinsk)
- Liga Bolchevique Internacionalista.Quarta Internacional
- Liga Socialista Revolucionaria (Unificada con Liga Marxista) (Argentina)
- LRCI League for a Revolutionary Communist International
- Maoist Internationalist Movement (MIM)
- Marxist Labour Party (Russia)

- Marksist Leninist Komunist Partisi (MLKP)
- Marxismo en Mexico
- Marxist Declaration and Summary ! For Marxist-L: eninist Unity
- Marxist-Leninist Party of Germany
- MAS Movimiento al Socialismo. Seccion Argentina de la LIT-CI (Liga Internacional de los Trabajadores-Cuarta Internaciona)
- Militant Socialist Organization (Austrailia)
- Militant Links (Vlandern, Belgium)
- MIR Movimiento de Izquierda Revolucionaria (Chile)
- MLPC Marxist-Leninist Party of Canada
- MLPD Marxistisch-Leninistische Partei Deutschlands
- MLPD Unigruppe Stuttgant
- MUNK'ASPART (Hungarian Worker's Party)
- National Democratic Front of the Philippines
- New Communist Party of Britain
- New Union Party
- New York State Communist Party
- Nucleo Marxista Hilo Rojo (HR)
- Offensief
- On MAI-Agreement (in danish)
- Organization of Revolutionary Workers of Iran (Rahe-Kargar)
- Organization of Socialista Internacional
- Organization Socialista Internacional (Puerto Rico)
- Pagina van de Gentse cellen van Militant
- Partei fur Soziale Gleichhert
- Parti Communiste Francais
- Partido Bolocheveque por la Cuarta Internacional
- Partido Comunista Brasileiro
- Partido Comunista de Andalucia
- Partido Comunista de Argentina
- Partido Comunista de Cuba
- Partido Comunista de Euskadi
- Partido Comunista do Brasil
- Partido Comunista en la Republic Dominicana

- Partido Comunista Marxista Lenisista del Ecuador (PCMLE)
- Partido Comunista Peruano
- Partido Comunista Portugues
- Partido Comunista Revolucionario de la Argenina
- Partido de la Revolucion Socialisa
- Partido de Trabajadores por el Socialismo (PTS)
- Partido dos Trabajo
- Partido dos Trabalhadores
- Partido Obrero Revolucionario
- Partido Popular Socialista
- Partido Popular Socialista –Marxista Leninista (Mexico)
- Partido Revolucionario Deominicano
- Partido Socialista de Chile
- Partido Socialista de los Trabajadores
- Partido Socialista del Uruguay
- Partido Socialista dos Trabalhadores Unificado
- Parti de l'egalite socialiste (Canada)
- Parti du Travail de Belgique
- Partido Bolchevique por la IV Internacional (Argentina)
- Partido Comunista (Marxista-Leninista) en la Republica Dominicana
- Partido Comunista Andaluz-Alcala de Guadaira
- Partido Comunista Brasileiro PCB
- Partido Comunista de Andalucia (Almeria)
- Partido Comunista de Argentina
- Partido Comunista de Castilla-Leon
- Partido Comunista de Cuba
- Partido Comunista de Espana (reconstitudio)
- Partido Comunista de Euskadi – Euskadiko Partidu Komunmista
- Partido Comunista de los Pueblos de Espana
- Partido Comunista de Turquia
- Partido Comunista do Brisil PcdoB
- Partido Comunista Japones JCP
- Partido Comunista Portuges PCP
- Partido Comunista Revoucionario (Argentina)

- Partido Comunista Virtual
- Partido de la Revolucion Socialist (Argentina)
- Partido del Trabajo (Mexico)
- Partido del Trabajo de Belgica
- Partido Obrero (Argentina)
- Partido Obrero Revolucionario (POR) Argentina)
- Partido Revolucionario de los Trabajadores (PRT)
- Partido Socialista des Trabalhadores Unificado (PSTU)
- Partido Socialista Revolucionario (PSR)
- Partit Dels Comunistes de Catalunya
- Partit Socialista Unificat de Catalunya
- Partito Comunisa Internazionalista (Battaglia Comunista)
- Partit Comunista del Pais Valencia PCPV
- Partit dels Comunistes de Catalunya PCC
- Partito Comunista Internationalista
- Partito della Rifondazione Comunista
- Partiya Sosyalist a Kurdistan (PSK)
- Party van de Arbeid van Belgie
- PCTP-MRPP Partido Comunista dos Trabalhadores Portugese
- Programa del Partido Comunista Marxista-Leninista (revolucionario)
- Progressive Labor Party
- PTS Partido de los trabajadores por el Socialismo (Argentina)
- Radical Society Artearoa
- Rattvisepartiet Socialisterna I Kiruma
- Reading Socialist Party
- Rebell.Jugendvenbandder Marxistisch-Leninistische Partei Deutschlands
- Red Youth Denmark
- Rete dei Communisti Unitari
- Revolution Youth
- Revolutionar Sozialistischer Bund/IV Internationale (RSB)
- Revolutionary Communist Party of Britain (Marxist-Leninist)

- Revolutionary Internationalist Movement
- Revolutionary Platform of the Socialist Labour Party
- Revolutionary Komsomol (Russia and Ukraine) RYCL(b)
- Revolutionary Peoples Liberation Struggle in Turkey (DHKP-C)
- Revolutionary Platform of the Socialist Labour Party
- Revolutionary Workers League U.S.A.
- RKU Revolutionar Kommunistisk Ungodom
- ROD UNGDOM
- ROD VALALAINSE (Red Election Alliance. Norway)
- Rote Fahne
- SACP South African Communist Party
- SAV Socialestische Alternative. Stadtverband Berlin
- SAV Sozialistische Alternative
- Secretariado Centro Americano del Centro Interacional del Trotskismo Ortodoxo
- Socialest Action
- Socialismo Internacional
- Socialist Appeal Harxist Voice of the Labour Movement
- Socialist Equality Party (Austrailia)
- Socialist Equality Party (Britain)
- Socialist Equality Party SEP/PES (Canada)
- Socialist Party
- Socialist Party - Reading
- Socialist Party in Ireland
- Socialist Worker Student Society (SWSS)
- **Socialist Workers Party**
- Socialist Workers Party (Britain)
- Socialist Workers Party (Ireland)
- Socialist Workers Party (Japan)
- Socialist Workers Party (Mauritius)
- Socialist Workers Party (Japan)
- Socialist Worker Student Society

- Socialisticka Solidarita (Gech Republic)
- Socialistische Party, thuisbasis van de Nederlandse Socialisten
- Socialistiska Partiet (Sweden)
- Socialistiska Partiet Goteborg
- Socialististk Folkerparty
- Song og Raud Valallianse Fjordane
- Solidarity
- Students for Socialist Action
- Sveriges Kommunistiska Parti
- The Communist Party of Canada
- The Communist-Left
- The Fourht International
- Ghe Guelph Socialist
- The International Brigades
- International Bureau for the Revolutionary Party (IBRP)
- The International Communist League
- The International Socialist Organization/Socialist Workers Party
- The Internationalist Group
- The Portuguese Communist Party PCP
- The Socialist Future Group
- **The World Socialist**
- Tribuna de los Trabajadores
- Trotskyist League U.S.
- Tudeh Party of Iran
- Turkiye Birlesik Komunist Partisi (TBKP)
- Turkiye Komunist Emek Partisi/Leninist
- Turkiye'de Marksist-Leninist Parti
- Turkiye'nin Istedigi Komunist Partisi
- Ung Socialisterna (Young Socialists Sweden)
- Unidad Obrea y Socialista (Mexic)
- UCE Unification Comunista de Espana
- Underground revolution
- Union Comunista Internacionalista
- **Union Comuniste Internationaliste**
- Union do Povo Galego
- Unione Comunista Internazionalista

- United Communists
- United Communists of America
- United Workers Party
- University of Toronto Communist Club
- **Vassar College Young Socialists**
- Workers Communist Party
- Workers Party of Belgium
- Worker-Communist Party of Iran
- Workers Party of Ireland
- Workers Party of New Zealand
- **Workers Party of USA**
- **World Socialist Movement**
- **World Socialist Party (New Zealand)**
- **World Socialist Party of the United States**
- **Young Communist League**
- Young Communist League U.S.A.
- Young Communist League – Minnesota
- Young Socialist
- **Young Socialist League**

- ADDENDUM IV –

A PLEA TO POLITICIANS

Please put a stop to mortgage lenders charging usurious interest rates of over ninety-percent in the first five years of the loan (Bank Mortgage Rate Table). In most states, the civil statutes dictate a ceiling on lending interest rates of between twenty-two percent and twenty-five percent. Credit card companies cannot charge usurious rates nor can loan sharks. To do so would be against the law, and severe criminal action would be taken by the State Attorney General and local law enforcement if the unlawful transaction was exposed. Why then can mortgage lenders (usually banks) collect interest payments of ninety-percent and higher in the first five to seven years of the mortgage? This abuse of power keeps people from paying off their mortgages and living mortgage free because they usually sell their house or refinance their mortgage within five to seven years of purchase (Monstermoving.com 2).

Example: House cost: $85,000 Mortgage Life: 30 years **Annual alleged interest rate: 8%**			
Years	**Cumulative Principal Paid[12]:**	**Cumulative Interest Paid[13]:**	**Actual Interest Rate Pd.:**
5	$4,290	$33,231	89%
Example: $4,290 + $33,231 = $37,521 paid to the mortgage lender. $33,231 ÷ $37,521 = 88.6% actual interest rate.			

[12] Amortization Calculator.com. pp. 1 & 3.

[13] Ibid.

[14] Mosnstermoving.com. Page 2.

So, if you sell your house after 5 years the principal reduces from $80,000 to only $75,710 ($80,000 – $4,290 in principal payments = $75,710 still due the bank = 88.6 percent was paid in interest). And keep in mind that most people statistically sell their homes within 5 –7 years due to divorce, financial problems, relocation, or upgrade[14].

I don't like government intervention into the private sector, but our society could use some help here. The enforcement of existing usury laws against mortgage lending companies would help citizens pay off their homes, become debt free, and then spend the balance of their life engaged in loftier pursuits than bill payment. This common sense enforcement of existing usury laws would financially help all classes of people and it would free up individual purchasing power that would, in turn, significantly stimulate the economy. If government officials better regulated unscrupulous U.S. mortgage lending institutions, it would be a landslide victory for the majority. Don't let the banks tie up all our money in usurious mortgage interest rate payments of eighty-nine to ninety-nine percent that are effectively devoid of principal loan reduction results. I don't care if the mortgage institutions and banks collude to call this amortization or shamitorization, --IT IS WRONG and should be stopped.

-ADDENDUM V –

A PLEA TO THE PRESS: IS IT FAIR THAT SOME CAN RETIRE AT AGE 55? ALSO: WE DO HAVE A NATIONAL HEALTH CARE PROGRAM.

I will be working until the age of sixty-seven years before I can retire. –This is because I worked in the private sector all of my life. Most of the readers of this mini-novel will also only be able to retire after they reach the age of sixty-seven. But, **New York State workers can retire at age fifty (New York State Teachers Retirement System 3). U.S. Military personnel may retire at only thirty-eight years of age**

(U.S. Military: Understanding Retirement Pay 2). And Federal employees may retire as early as age fifty under the 'early out' program (United States Office of Personnel Management 7 & 42). So while these retired workers lay around for seventeen to twenty-nine years watching soap operas, we (the taxpayers) must hire others to do their jobs. This is ridiculous. It costs us double in benefits and wage payments, it is unnecessary, and it is wasteful. But what's more troubling, is that these retired State and Federal workers can vote on issues that cost New York State residents tax money while **they are not taxed on their New York State pension earnings or social security retirement earnings**. *(Note: The private sector **does pay the full {typical} 8.5 percent state income tax on their pension/retirement earnings** after the first $20,000 in income received but New York State workers and Federal workers residing in New York State pay ZERO State taxes against their retirement income).* This system ensures ample 'YES' votes from all New York State retired workers and New York State resident retired Federal workers for New York State projects that are presented for a vote. Why shouldn't they vote for their union backed public/state spending program, when it costs this group of retirees nothing to do so? This system is extremely corrupt, and the news media should constantly expose this inequity and corruption. If a privately owned United States corporation pulled a stunt like this, the press would be all over the story crying 'foul', but because our government is involved many reporters stick to their standard 'hands off' policy. We have changed from a capitalistic society to a socialistic society that is rapidly migrating toward a communistic society (government dominated and government run) and very few seem aware of this progression and eventuality. Worse yet, only a select few news reporters will report on this corrupt situation because they to are controlled by their union, and to expose union corruption and excesses would subject them to probable retaliation.

Also, it would be nice if the press more aptly acknowledged that **we do have** substantial and active National Health Care programs in the United States. These programs go by the names of 'Medicare', 'Medicaid', The Federal Prison Healthcare System, and State Children's Health Insurance Program (SCHIP). While it is fine to argue that we may want to expand these current national healthcare programs, please stop pretending that they don't already exist. In 1999, the nation spent $264 billion on Medicare for elderly and retired persons (Geriatric Times 2) and $1,125 billion on Medicaid for indigent and disabled persons (Stashenko.6). The typical 1999 New York State Medicaid beneficiary received $20,767 in Medicaid dollars (Hanys 5) and $7,898 was the average Medicare beneficiary payment (Thorpe 2). Additionally, in 1999 there were well over 2 million inmates our Federal prison system, illegal immigrant Federal detention centers, state prisons, and county jails. (Bureau of Justice Statistics 1, Federal Bureau of Prisons 1, CBS News 2). They all received 100 percent free health care as part of our current Department of Corrections and Department of Immigration 'National Health Care Program'. Mental patients in all county, state, or Federally run psychiatric facilities are also covered under a nationally and locally funded healthcare program if their families cannot contribute. So to suggest that we don't have a National Health Care Program already in place is ridiculous, absurd, and a lie.

From each paycheck recipient, 1.5 percent is taken out for the Medicare program. If they earn over $100,000 per year, the paycheck recipient will pay 2.5 percent of his/her gross income. The Medicaid program is paid for out of our typical 8.5 percent New York income tax fund. While liberals like Hillary Clinton and Ted Kennedy want to liberally spend more of taxpayers' money on these current (in place) programs, please don't let them get away with pretending that a National Health Care system doesn't already exist. Make them state that they want to spend more on the existing programs vs. using their mantra that they are "inventing" a National Health Care system as if it weren't already in place. Please challenge government politicians on the facts as opposed to continuously writing info-commercials for them. Also, do your homework and tell us what each of the individual politicians' plans will cost **each** taxpayer in the United States, above what they're already paying . Reporters need to dig much deeper into their stories, and they need to become less concerned with offending the union that they and their employer are members of while becoming more concerned with the thorough and honest reporting of hard and irrefutable facts. Reporters should site more quantitative statistics and less subjective interviews (baseless opinions) in their stories.

U.S. Population Trends
1999

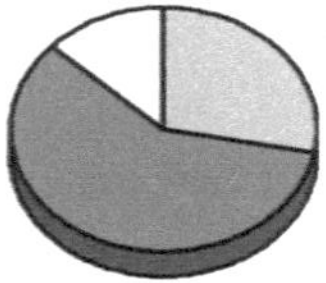

Age 67-UP
13%

Age 0-17
28%

Age 18-66
59%

U.S. Population Trends
2025

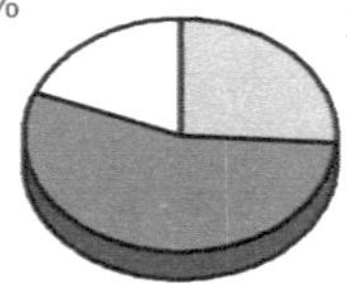

Age 67-UP
19%

Age 0-17
26%

Age 18-66
55%

(Source: The above estimates and projections were derived from the U.S. Census Bureau. "Population Projections Program Statistics." Jan. 13, 2000.).

As our population base of retired persons increases 46% (from 13% to 19% of our total U.S. population), those left working will be required to foot the extra Medicaid and Medicare costs. To help ease the strain on working families, we should not be required to pay Medi care benefits for retirees that can afford to pay for their own medical expenses.

- ADDENDUM VI –

HOW WOULD YOU REACT DURING A NUCLEAR DISASTER?

During a power plant failure or a military attack, would you know how to react to protect yourself and your loved ones?

THE ADVERSE AFFECTS OF NUCLEAR RADIATION EXPOSURE.	
< 2/10 of a roentgen per year, possesses	No adverse affect. This represents the typical level of "background" nuclear radiation that is always surrounding us and possesses no impending threat. This level is too low to be measured by the kinds of radiological instruments used during a nuclear disaster where levels would be thousands of times higher and would be measured in roentgens per hour (R/hr).
5—49 R (Roentgen per hour)	•Loss of appetite and nausea. Blood cells change at 5 R.
50R—200 R	**DEATH FOR 5%:**
	•Damage to the immune system's ability to fight disease. •Skin burns (1st, 2nd, *md* 3^ degree), •Skin itching and burning sensations. •Loss of hair in 2 weeks. •Radiation sickness. •Probable death rate = less than 5% of those exposed will begin dying in 60 days or more.
201R—450 R	**DEATH FOR UP TO 49%:**
	•Probable death rate = up to 49% of those exposed will begin dying in 30 days or more.
451R—600 R	**DEATH FOR MORE THAN 50%:**
	•Probable death rate = more than 50% of those exposed will begin dying in 30 days or more.

600 **R**	**•DEATH FOR ALL**
	•Catastrophic death will occur within a short two week period.
	Source: Federal Emergency Management Agency Manual entitled, "Radiation Safety in Shelters: A handbook for finding and providing the best protection in shelters with the use of instruments for detecting nuclear radiation." Sept., 23, 1983. pp. CPG2-6.4 1-7 CH.l-8c.

APPENDIX C

RADIATION PEN DOSIMETER MEASUREMENT DEVISE

PEN DOSIMETER

For Measuring: Gamma Radiation
X-Ray Radiation

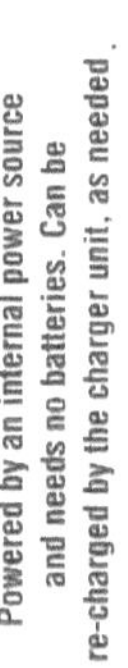

Powered by an internal power source and needs no batteries. Can be re-charged by the charger unit, as needed .

PEN DOSIMETER ILLUMINATION LIGHT

(Optional)

Powered by 2 AA batteries.

PEN DOSIMETER CHARGER

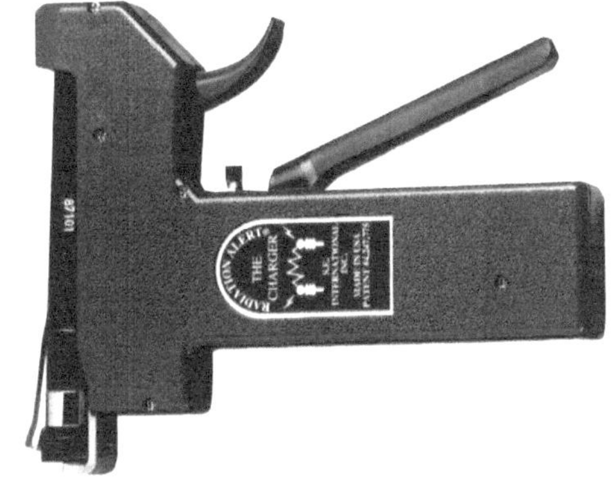

Powered by an internal piezoelectric power source. Needs no batteries or electric outlet.

APPENDIX D

RADIATION PORTABLE ALARM DOSIMETER MEASUREMENT DEVISE

PORTABLE ALARM DOSIMETER

With digital display.

(Newer/advanced model to the traditional "pen" detector).

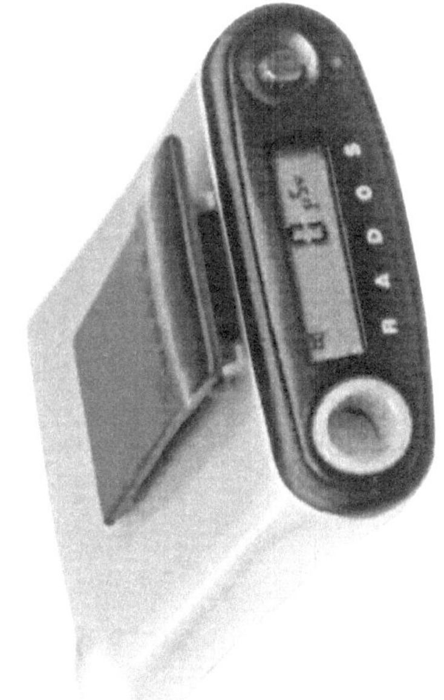

For Measuring:
Gamma Radation
X-Ray Radation

- Alarm Sounds when a pre-set radiation level is detected.

Powered by 1 "AAA" battery.

APPENDIX E

RADIATION SURVEY METER MEASUREMENT DEVISE

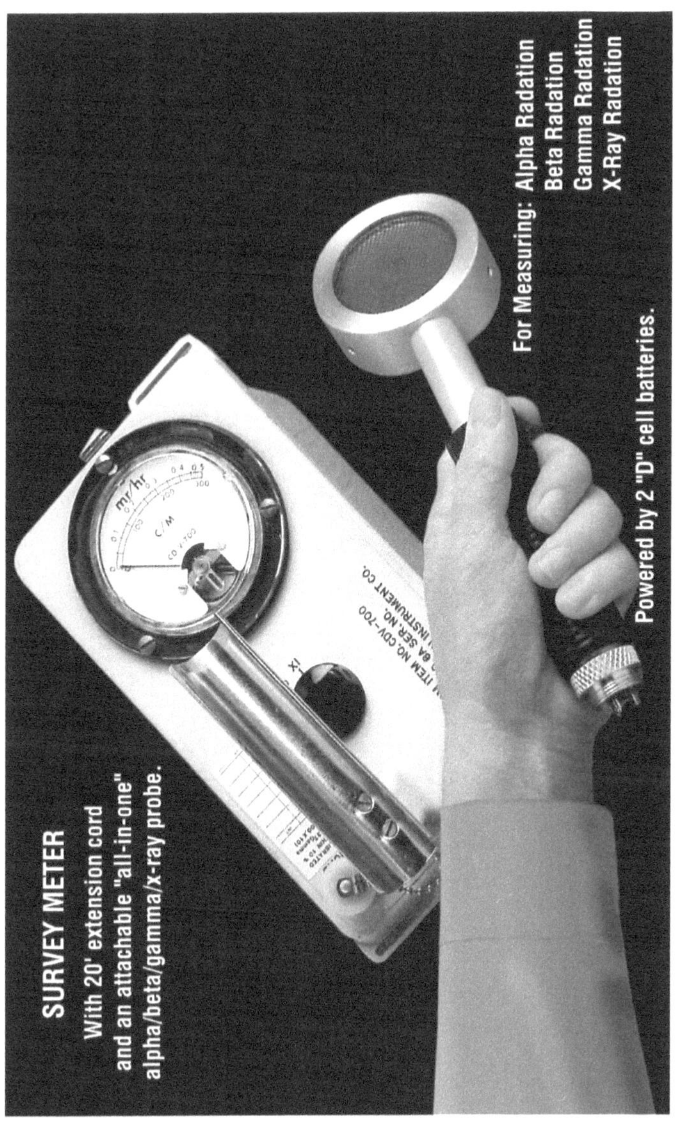

APPENDIX F

FALLOUT SHELTER COVER, LATCH, AND REAR VIEW SCHEMATIC.

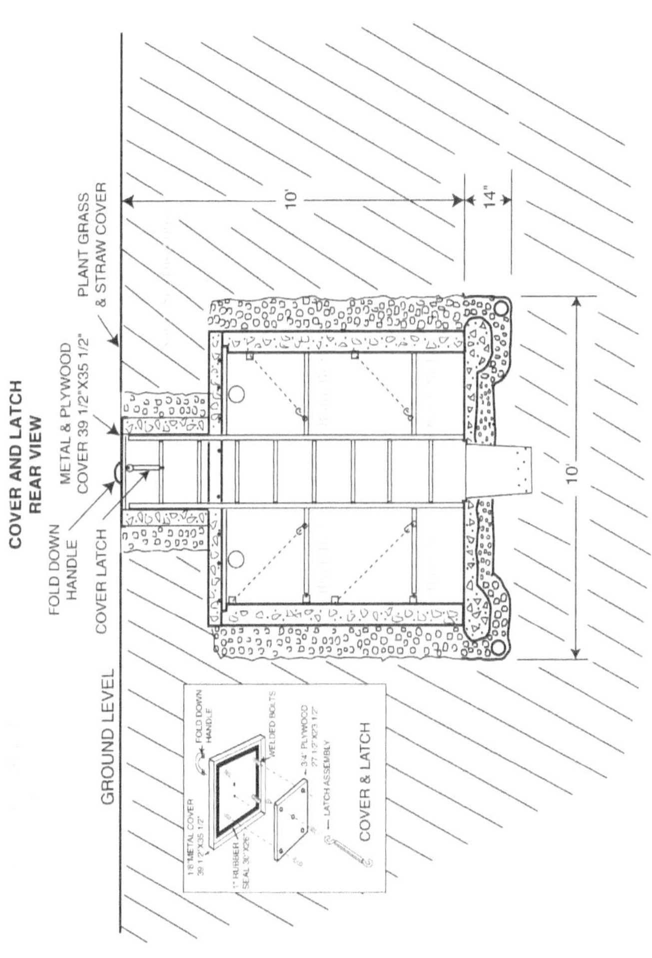

APPENDIX G

FALLOUT SHELTER SIDE VIEW SCHEMATIC

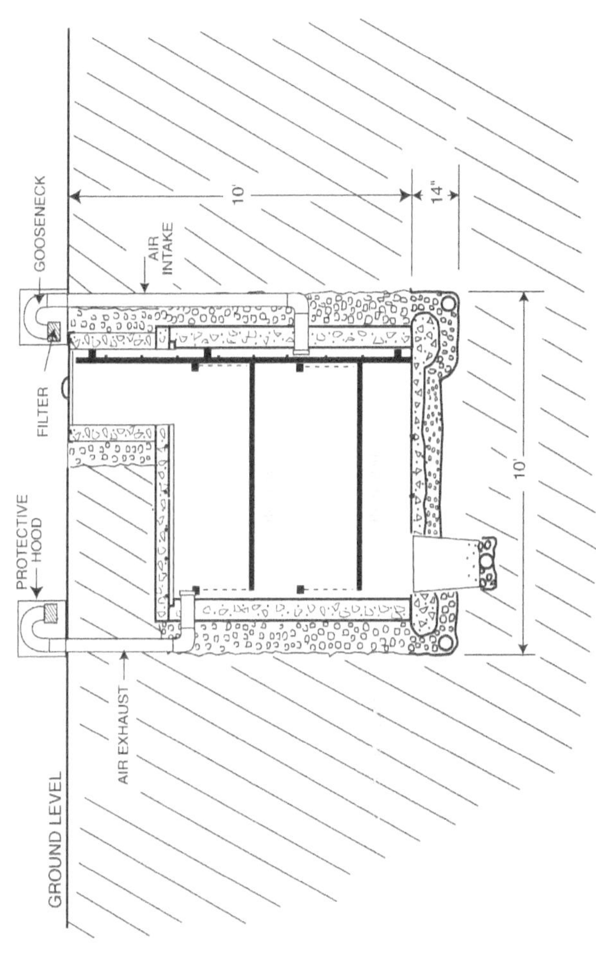

APPENDIX H

HAND CRANK BLOWER PHOTO

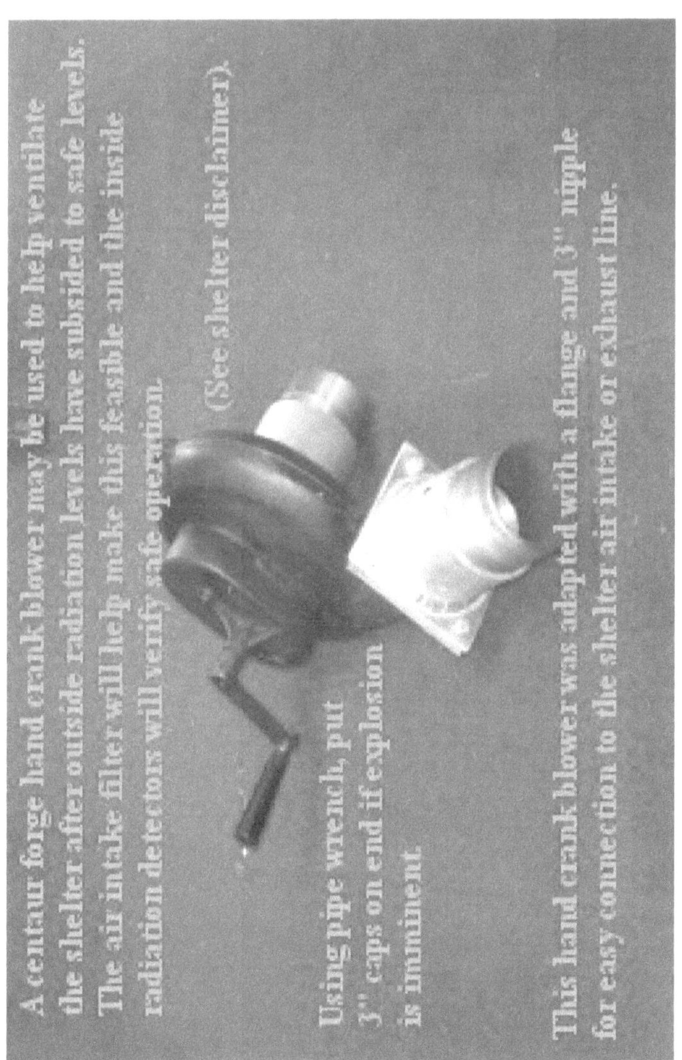

APPENDIX I

POTASSIUM IODIDE PILLS

Potassium Iodide Pills:

Potassium Iodide pills can help the thyroid block the absorption of harmful radioactive iodine in the event of radiation emergencies. This may significantly reduce the risk of thyroid cancer in humans during time of nuclear emergency. These pills may be marketed in various trade names, but the basic component is potassium iodide. Read the manufacturer's recommendations and safety data sheet before using. These pills may be packaged in a small plastic bottle or foil wrapped dispenser pouches.

(Source: FDA, EPA, NRC, Dept. of Health and Human Services, and American Thyroid Association).

(See Fallout Shelter Disclaimer).

-ADDENDUM VII –

FALLOUT SHELTER DESIGN DISCLAIMER.

The previous fallout shelter ideas are to be used for educational purposes only and neither the author nor publisher assumes legal liability. **If you build a shelter, it is recommended that you consult an engineering, engineering design, and construction firm that is licensed to practice in your state and is familiar with the local zoning and building codes.** We also recommend that you take your final design to your local Federal Emergency Management Agency to see if any updated information should be added to your design before construction.

Additionally, while the previous shelter ideas are useful in planning the design of your personal fallout shelter, don't forget that most communities have public shelters available as well. Please be aware of where your closest public shelter is located. **But most of all, be educated and be prepared!**

Works Cited

Bender, Frederich L. Karl Marx: The Communist Manifesto. New York: Norton Company, 1988. pp. 63, 74, 86.

Bill Gates Salary. p 2 (1999). www.boardoptions.com/ychightechsalary.htm

Bill Gates Donations. p.1 (1999) www.ananova.com/business/story/sm 331680.html?menue" www.trust.gatesscholar.org/about.asp www.gatesfoundation.org/Education/SmallHighSchools/Announcements/Announce-0 www.buzzle.com/editorials/text9-24-1999-45827.asp www.search.biography.com/print_record.pl?id=15061

Boeing 747, Internet, (1998). www.flugrevuedatafiles: BoeingVC-25A www.cnn.com/1998/US/10/22/airforece.one/ www.HW#15107-AirforeceOneBoeing 747Airplane.com www.BoeingVC-25A-AirForceone.com www.Military-Aircraft-VC-25A.com www.Boeing747.com

Bureau of Justice Statistics. Prison Statistics. Washington, DC: Bulletin. Dec. 1999.

CBS News. "More Inmates, Less Cash." July 2001. www.cbsnews.com/stories/2001/04/07/nataional/main548143.shtml

Cortland Savings Bank, Mortgage Rate Computation Tables. Cortland, New York. 1999.

Encarta Standard Encyclopedia. The Communist Manifesto, CD-ROM. Redmond, WA. Microsoft Corporation. p. 1. 1999.

Federal Bureau of Prisons. Federal Bureau of Prisons QUICK FACTS. Nov. 1999 Bulletin. Also: www.bop.gov/'fact0598.html#population

Forbes Magazine. Survey of the 400 Wealthiest Americans. New York: March 1999. p. 23

Forbes Magazine. Fortune 500 Companies. New York: December 1999. p. 37

Geriatric Times. Is there a formula for Funding Seniors' Prescription Drug Benefit? Minneapolis, MN: CME, Inc. December 2002, Vol. III, Issue 6, p. 2.

HANYS. Healthcare Association of New York State. Rensselaer, NY: 1999 Bulletin p.5. Also: www.hanys.org/Sound ApproachReport.pdf

Hutchings, Robert Maynard. Great Books of the Western World: The Communist Manifesto. New York: Encyclopedia Britannica Books, Inc. 1984. p. 429.

IRS (Internal Revenue Service). "IRS Statistics 1999". (1999). www.beta1.bizjournals.com/wichita/stores/1999/12/20/story3.html

IRS. "IRS Statistics of Income Bulletin". Washington, DC. (1999). www.mckenzielaw.com/auditsta.html www.unclefed.com/Tax-News/1999nr99-55.html

James, Andrew. The Song, The Best Poets of 2001, International Library of Poetry, Owings Mills, MD: Watermark Press. (1999): p.50.

Jet Fuel, Various Internet Sites, 1998. www.zoomoon.co.uk/ba747etra.html www.britishairways.com/flights/factfile/airfleet/docs/y7472.shtml

"Microsoft 1999 Annual Report/Corporate Income Statement." (1999). www.Microsoft.com/msft/ar99/downloads/ar99.doc

Monstermoving.com. "10 Minutes with a Mortgage Expert."

1999. P. 2. www.google.com/search?Q=Average+Mortgage +Lenth+&hl=en&IR=880e=utf-8&Start

MPI Home Video: Air Force One: Flight II. Dayton, OH: Elliott Sluhan Productions Video Cassette 1991.

National Veterans Affairs and Rehabilitation Commission. Deaths in Service of Those Who Have Served in America's Wars and Conflicts. Washington, D.C.: The American Legion Bulletin, April 1997.

"New York State Teacher's Retirement System." (2001): p. 3. www.nystrs.org/main/2001egpro.html#Tier=%20Equity

"OPIC (Overseas Private Investment Corporation)." (1998). www.gao.gov/new.terms/ms00159b.pdf www. foreignpolicy-infocus.org/brief/wl4/v-4n19opic_body.html www.house.gov/budget/waste/wateexamples.htm

"Russia Foreign Aid." (1998). www.Shaps.hawaii.edu/ economic/opic-russia.html www.gao.gov/new.terms/ ms00159b.pdf

Stashenko, Joel. Medicade Bedevils State, Local Budget Writers. Cortland, N.Y.: Cortland Standard Newspaper, November 15, 2003. p. 6

Stybel, Peabody, & Associates, Inc. "Trends in High Tech Compensation: Salary Survey- Executive compensation/ Bill Gates." www.boardoptions.com/ychightechsalary.htm

"The Budget for Fiscal Year 1998." Washington, DC: Federal Budget Office. 1998. pp. 249 & 262. Also: html:// w3.access.gpo.gov/usbudget/fy1998/pfd/budget.pfd

"The Economic Support Fund.": 1998. www.wizardsofmoney. org/wiz12/state-esf.htm www.stategov/documents/ organization/17230.pdf

"The Federal Budget for Fiscal Year 1998." Washington, DC: Federal Budget Office. p. 23.

The Federal Government Dollar Fiscal Year 1999 Estimates. Washington, DC: Budget Office Report. 1999.

"The Population of the United States: 1815-1998." January 1 (1999): p. 1. www.mste.uiuc.edu/malcz/ExpFit/data.html

The Ryrie Study Bible, King James Version. Chicago, IL: Moody Press. 1976. p. 1373 (Matthew 19:24).

"The State Department Economic Support Fund." pp. 1-6. (1999). www.wizarsofmoney.org//wiz12/State-esp.htm

The United States Constitution: To provide for calling forth the Militia to execute the Laws of the Union, suppress Insurrections and repel Invasions. Article I, Section 8, Clause 15. www.house.gov/Constitution/Constitution.html. Also: Washington, DC.: The United States Constitution. 1999.

Thorpe, Kennith E. Medicare Typical Cost per Beneficiary. Atlanta, Ga.: Emory University Press 1999. p.1

U.S. Census Bureau. Resident Population of the United States. January 1 (1999): pp. 4-4. www.census.gov/population/estimates/nation/intfile2-1.txt Also: Washington, DC: U.S. Census Bureau Report on Resident Population of the United States. pp. 1-4. 1999.

U.S. Census Bureau. "The First U.S. census completed in 1790." August 1, (1998): pp. 1-3. www.burger.com/august.htm

U.S. Census Bureau. “The United States in 1810.” January 1, (1999): p.1 www.cnesusresearch.com/1810map.htm

U.S. Military. “Understanding Military Retirement Pay.” January 5, (1999): p. 2. www.usmilitary.about.com/cs/generalpay/a/retirementpay_4.htm

U.S. State Department. State Department Support Fund. Washington, DC.: State Department 1999 Annual Report. 1999. pp.1-2.

United States General Accounting Office. The Overseas Private Investment Corporation's Investment Funds Program. Washington, DC.: May 1999 Report. pp. 1-42.

United States Office of Personnel Management. Retirement Statistics. Washington, DC: Booklet. 1999. Also: www.opm/feddata/retire/rs-profices.pdf

ABOUT THE AUTHOR

Andrew James wrote this book to help express the views of millions of hard-working Americans whose voices would otherwise never be heard. For those who work the hardest in America lack the time to adequately convey their grievances against excessive taxation, while those who work the least possess ample time to enact governmental change at the expense of the producer.

James is a graduate of the State University of New York at Marcy where he graduated Magna Cum Laude with a degree in business management and marketing. His graduate work was completed at Syracuse University. He writes in the pseudonym to avoid government persecution for his views.

www.ingramcontent.com/pod-product-compliance
Lightning Source LLC
Chambersburg PA
CBHW030428290526
45786CB00001B/192

* 9 7 8 1 5 8 7 2 1 5 2 2 3 *